The Ceremonies of the Dragon Magic contained in this book are offered as a free download for easy printing. Visit http://qr.spiritualjourneys.com/Ceremonies-of-Dragon-Magic.pdf to download this file.

Secrets of Dragon Magic

Almine

The Sacred Fires of the Hadji-ka

Published by Spiritual Journeys LLC

Copyright June 2013

MAB 998 Megatrust
By Almine
Spiritual Journeys LLC
P.O. Box 300
Newport, Oregon 97365

US toll-free number: 1-877 552 5646

www.spiritualjourneys.com

All rights reserved. No part of this publication may be reproduced without crediting Almine as the author and originator of this material.

Cover Illustration - Chas Frizzell

Manufactured in the United States of America

ISBN Softcover 978-1-936926-56-5

ISBN Adobe Reader 978-1-936926-57-2

Table of Contents

Part I – The Philosophy of the Magic of the Nine Directions

Introduction 3
The Windows of the Magical Life 5
The Dragon Windows of the Magical Life 9
The Magical Practices of the 24 Wheels of Veshba
    and the Maps for Clearing the Nervous System 13
The Locations for the Maps of the Nervous System 71
The Dragon Affirmations for the Spine and Brain Stem 73
The Magical Practices of the 24 Wheels of Manasuch
    and The Wheels to Activate the Pure and Full Expression
    of the Kundalini 75
The Wheel of the Ninth Direction 139
The Magical Practices of the Wheels of Hurat 149

Part II – Practices of Dragon Magic

General Guidelines for Performing Ceremonies 185
The Ceremony to Clear Programs from the Spine 191
The Ceremony to Clear the Programs from the Pranic Tube 195
The Ceremony to Clear the Ida and Pingala – the Instruments
    of Spirit 201
The Ceremony to Restore the Missing Codes
    of the Four Directions 209
The Ceremony for the Fusion of the Four Directions 224
The Ceremony to Fuse the Combined Eight Directions
    with the Ninth Direction 234

Closing 239

Part III – The 144 Precepts of Higher Life
Precepts of the Path to Freedom 243
Precepts of the Body, Soul and Spirit 317
Precepts of the Mysteries of Existence 349
Precepts of the Embodiment of The Infinite 357

Closing 400

Part I

The Philosophy of the Magic of the Nine Directions

Introduction

The information given by the custodians of these sacred records, the dragons of Avondar, is life-altering in its scope and power. The magical life is as natural to them as breathing, requiring no learnt methodology.

The powerful influence of these sacred records is designed to restore the magic of man in two ways: Firstly by removing the blockages to these innate and natural abilities and secondly to enhance consciousness through increased perception. With increased consciousness comes increased resources and hence, also enhanced abilities.

The crux of the magical life is the reduction of the gap between cause and effect; between intent and manifestation. To achieve this, density has to be decreased. The removal of illusions can be called the main purpose of this book. It is also the key to magic by reducing density in our lives.

May these holy records and their groundbreaking revelations restore the precious heritage of man: A life of incorruptible white magic.

The Windows of the Magical Life

White magic is the ability to reduce the delay between cause and effect by accessing the indivisible essence within.

~ Almine

The Symbol for the 75 Wheels of Magic

The Sacred Fires of Hadji-ka
Transmissions from the Dragons

The Dragon Windows of the Magical Life

According to the ancient records of Hadji-ka, the magic of humans was lost when the spinal column separated from the pranic tube and the interaction between the prana and the nervous system was lost. There are 75 windows of alchemy, abilities presently dormant in man, that open within the spine when this interaction takes place.

There are three stages of resurrection. In the first, the body moves into the soul level and unites as one with its soul. This is different than death where the soul leaves for the soul level and the body is left behind to decay. This first stage can also take place when the soul, or dream-body, merges with the physical (as is described in the Bible as the resurrection of Christ).

The first stage, in which the feminine (soul) and masculine (body) become one, enables one to become free from life cycles (incarnation) and death cycles. But it is only in the second stage where one has the necessary power to move between the soul level and physical reality at will.

The second level of a resurrected master enables the magical abilities that once belonged to man, to be restored. White magic is the ability to reduce the delay between cause and effect by accessing the indivisible essence within.

The second level of a resurrected being occurs when the prana merges with the spinal column, precipitating the alchemical openings of inter-dimensional gateways in the spinal column. This again represents the merging of the feminine (prana) and masculine (nervous system).

The pranic tube is a straight tube which lies in the etheric dream-body that overlays the physical body and occupies the same space. At night, the dream-body travels into the parallel reality of the soul, attached by a silver cord to the physical body so that it can be called back when the physical body is awakened.

The pranic tube has the same circumference as your middle finger and thumb placed tip to tip to form a circle. It travels from the top of the head to the base of the spine, straight through the body. When it merges with the spinal column, it has to assume the same curvature as the spine.

The first prerequisite for this merging to take place is through the understanding of 75 very specific insights, which then yield the frequencies of the rapture of eternal romance in the joining of masculine and feminine.

Part I The Philosophy of the Magic of the Nine Directions

A Map of the 75 Alchemical Windows of the Nervous System That Open When the Prana and the Nervous System Merge

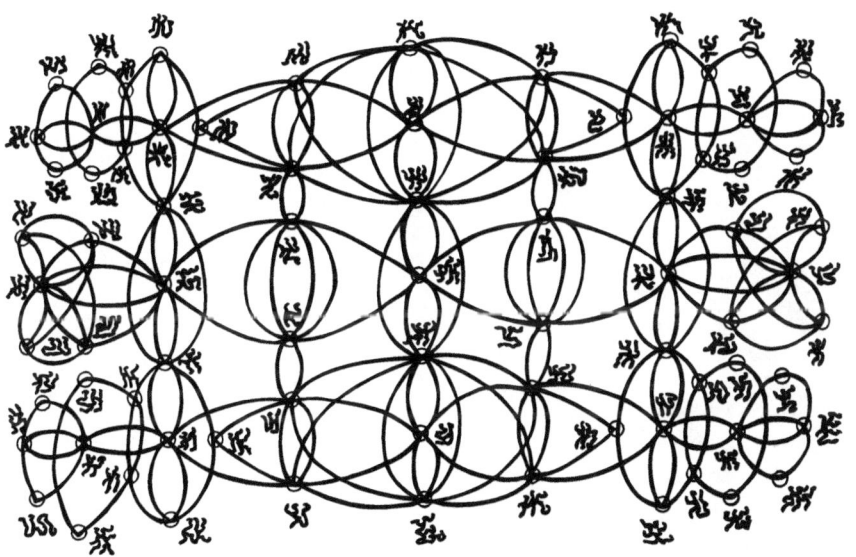

The Magical Practices of the 24 Wheels of Veshba

The Symbol for the Wheels of Veshba

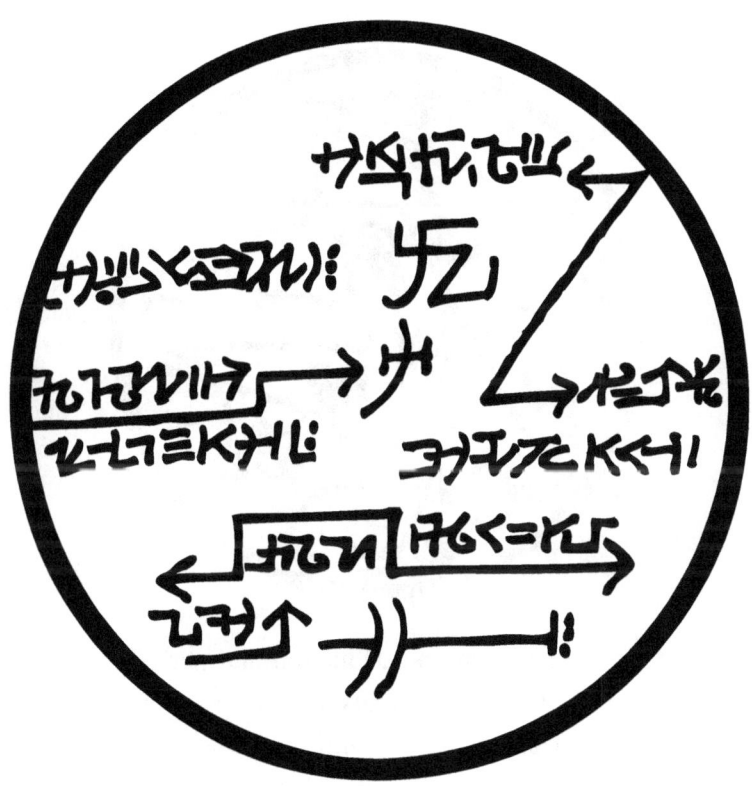

The 24 Wheels of Veshba
Insights for Opening the Dragon Gates

1. Birchsparet-hevenasvi

There are periods of reason and deduction and periods of effortless knowing of inevitability. The times of reason produce form and structure. The times of non-cognitive knowing produce fluid formlessness and destructuring. Jointly, they produce eternal moments and the gaps between the moments. Timelessness is produced by living them as one – knowing the inevitable and with reasoning, finding out why it is so.

Clearing the Central Nervous System Map 1

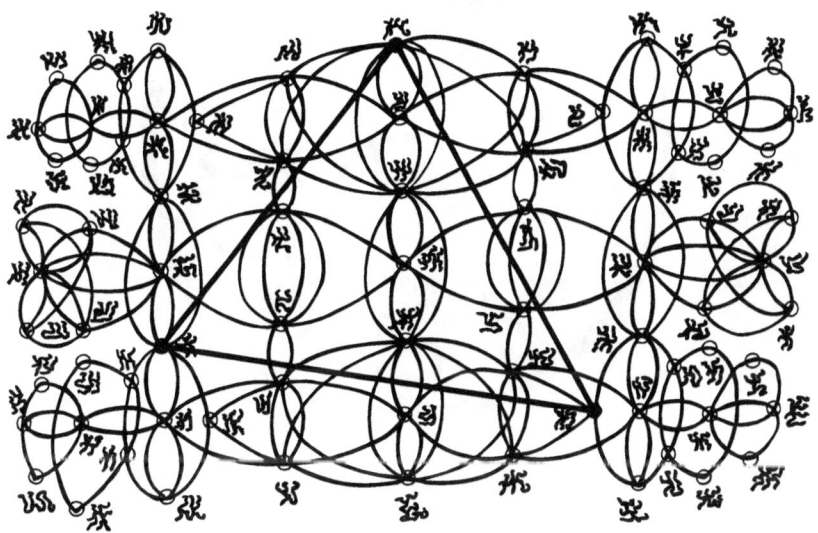

Incantation:
Nechpa-uhurares-minachvi-sursata

2. Blishbretbraha-avaneski

The feminine perspective does not like to be definitive and precise. The masculine on the other hand, thrives on it. The tendency to confuse and delay the conclusion of the masculine's plans and agendas has been seen by the masculine as being obstructive. The masculine's tendency to demand a controlled outcome has been seen by the feminine as controlling and dictatorial. In cooperative integration it must be appreciated that the feminine's lack of preciseness leaves gateways of higher possibilities open. It provides openings for alchemical leveraging into higher and unforeseen outcomes. The masculine conclusiveness allows this fluid potential to actualize into manifestation.

Clearing the Central Nervous System Map 2

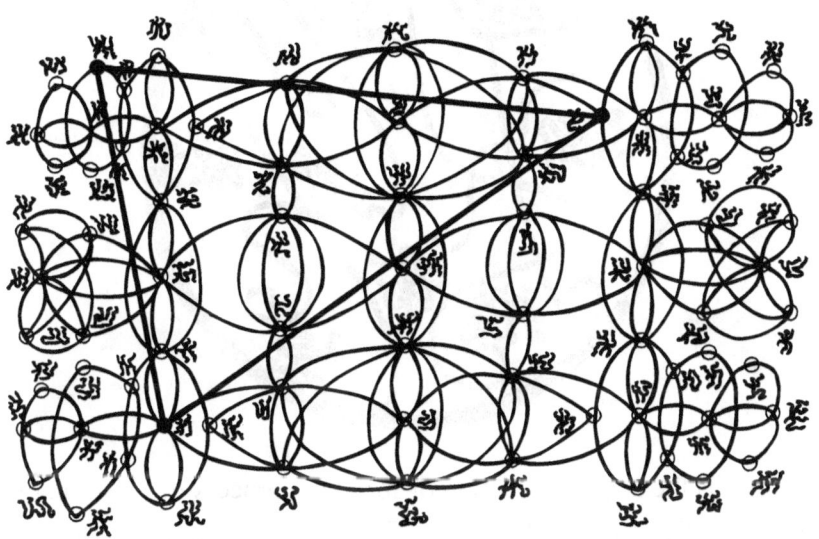

Incantation:

Esenach-misanat-hulspave-skiharsat-upreve

3. Michba-erenechspavi

Impurity is the stage of creation of form; the process of clustering the resources of existence into shapes. That which is interpreted as purity, is the release of the inner tension that maintains form. Impurity blocks the flow of unfolding existence and dams up resources to produce form. Impurity, from the heart's standpoint, is the linear movement of mind. From the mind's standpoint, it is the circular movement of emotion in a seemingly chaotic manner. As all opposites do, the one begets the other. They work together to produce fluid form – the playground of indivisible, Infinite existence.

Clearing the Central Nervous System Map 3

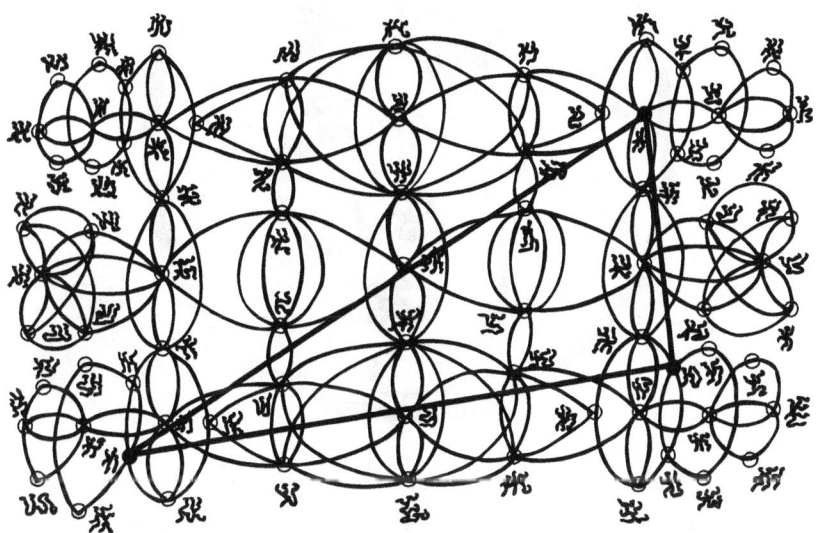

Incantation:
Klisa-aharavech-asetu-urat

4. Kuhu-uret-avastra

Honor is a mind-made concept that arises from the fact that the feminine has for eons suppressed itself so that the masculine could grow. Honor is the living of programmed protocols. In polarity, more of one pole is less of the other. The masculine's inner feminine and masculine has become whole and mature. The feminine has only its feminine pole functioning. This has made it unable to interpret its own experiences since the electrical, masculine component interprets the memories held by the feminine. The protection of honor is the masculine making sure that it protectively surrounds the feminine so that all experiences can be interpreted. It surrounds it by producing matrices that have to be continually produced as the feminine pushes beyond them - hence the search of the masculine to understand.

Clearing the Central Nervous System Map 4

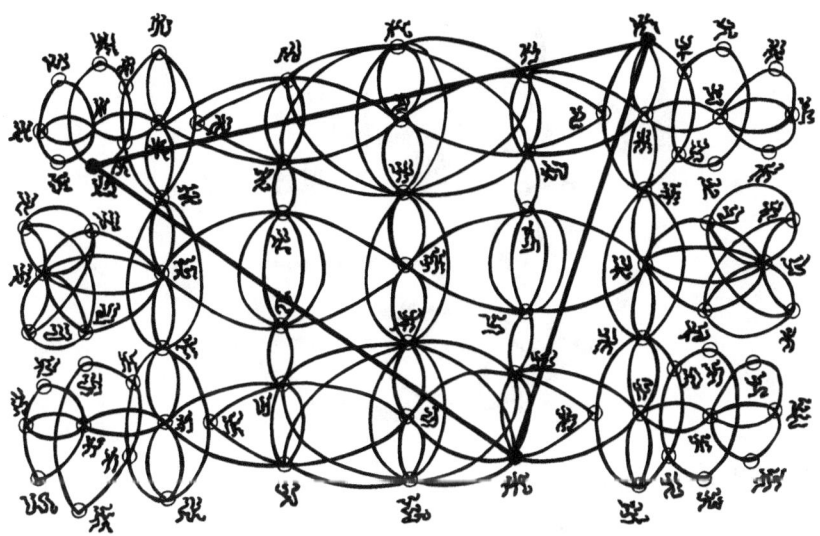

Incantation:

Skelparsaha-ninuset-bravech-spaha-hurasbi

5. Skuhu-ustrech-velesvi

The judgment of the masculine, seeing itself as responsible for the feminine which it sees as irresponsible, is because it does not see the larger perfection of how they work together. The masculine desires to contain, which the feminine interprets as control. The feminine desires to be free of boundaries, which the masculine interprets as irresponsible since she cannot interpret her experience when she leaves the boundaries of his interpretation. The way these opposing desires work together is that, the masculine (perception) keeps having to expand to match the expansion of the feminine (emotion) and in this way, the self is systematically explored; the unknown turned into the known through experience.

Clearing the Central Nervous System Map 5

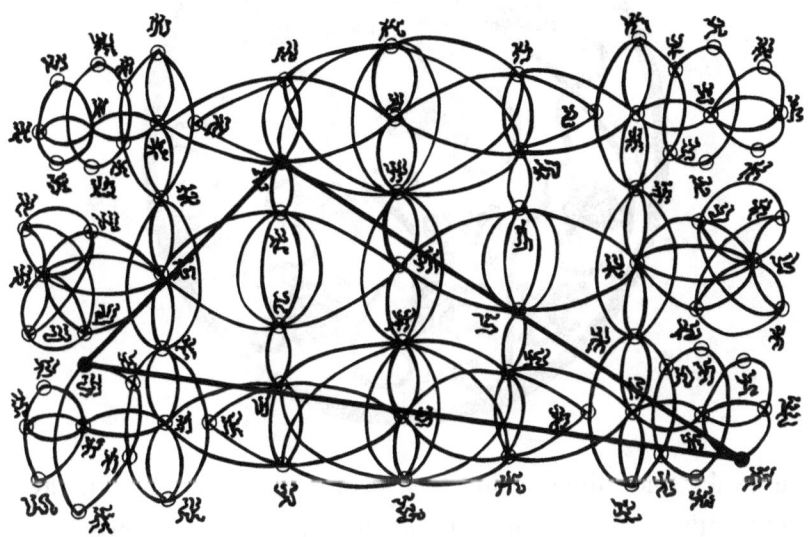

Incantation:
Bil-eshenet-eklet-vavi-hasuta-asanet

6. Spere-hespa-klubanet

The awake state (life's realm) has become more real than the dream state (death's realm) because it got stuck. This happened because the feminine, not understanding the value of its uninterpreted emotion, and feeling itself to be unwhole, lost the self-confidence of expression. Authentic impulses of expression should be regarded as valid, even if the perfection of the large picture cannot be seen.

Clearing the Central Nervous System Map 6

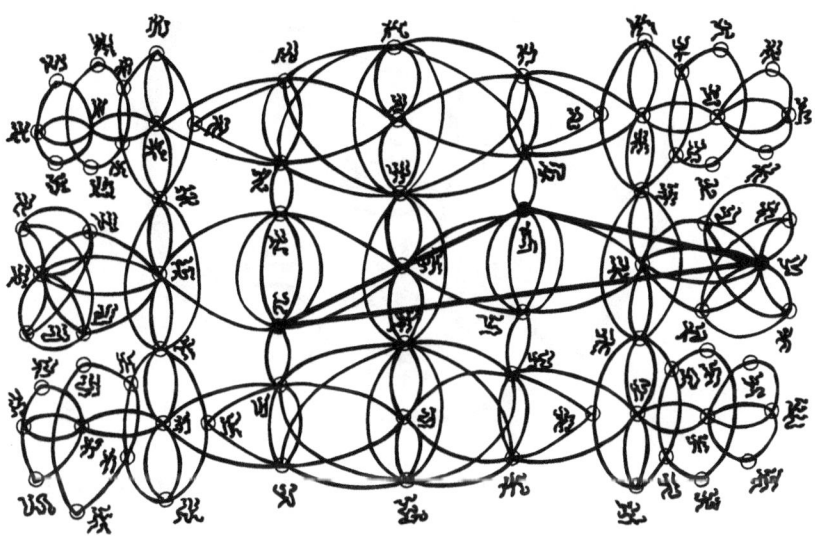

Incantation:

Pleshba-heruhit-servasva-unech-vi-varabit

7. Kerch-spibaresvi

The masculine is afraid of what it cannot control. The feminine is afraid of being controlled. It is this opposing agenda that creates the tension that sustains the cohesive form of the cosmos. The masculine provides form and the feminine provides growth. This creates the harmonious interplay of structure and flow.

Clearing the Central Nervous System Map 7

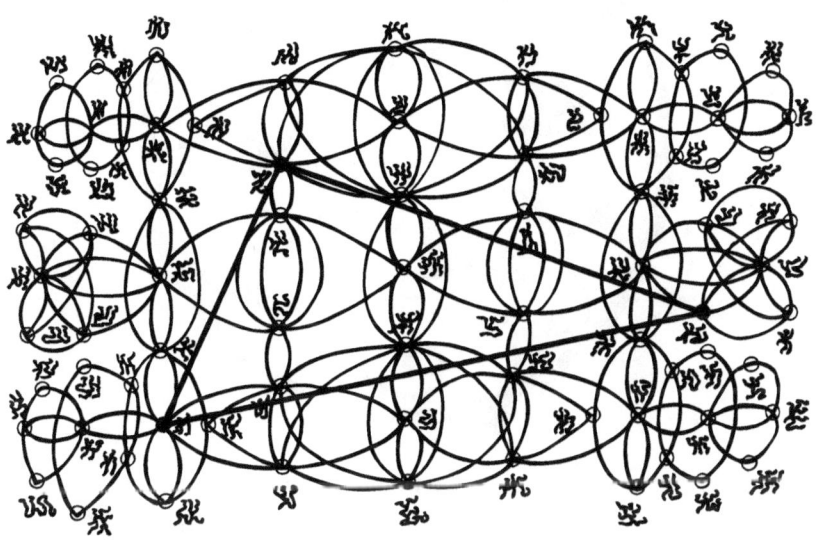

Incantation:

Kruves-aras-unasvi-brivabesbi-skrihunat

8. *Nichsta-erek-hursavi*

The masculine has lived the masculine pole and the feminine pole. The feminine became balanced when the Atlantean information of the 300 angels was released. Atlantis represented the masculine pole of the Earth – North America now represents it. The neutral pole (Western Europe +/– and Eastern Europe –/+), will be expressed by both when the 75 dragon windows yield their insights.

Part I The Philosophy of the Magic of the Nine Directions

Clearing the Central Nervous System Map 8

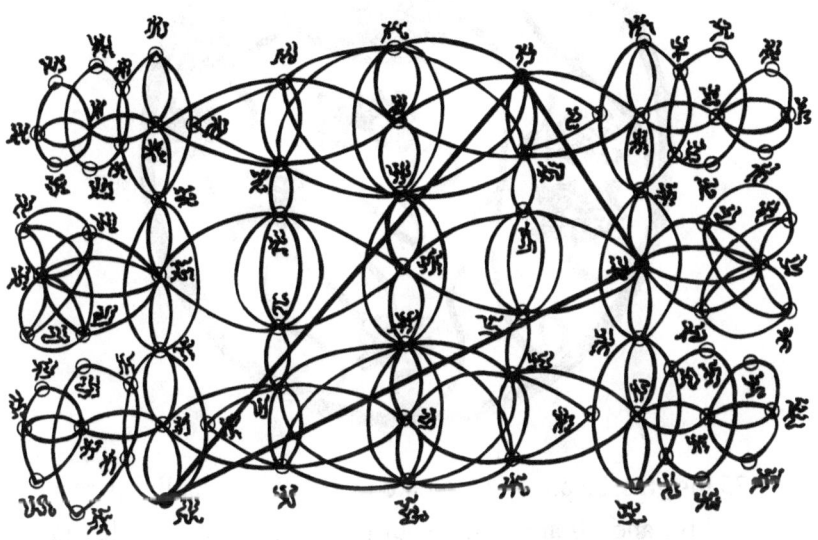

Incantation:

Birspa-eseklet-briherechspa-utre-minuveset

9. Mishba-ukret-ninusklat

Of the 75 insights, 25 are of the awake world (the masculine perception-based reality) and 50 are of the soul realms or dream world, and are non-cognitive realizations of the perfect harmonious interplay of the seeming opposition of the masculine and feminine. These insights jointly will allow the masculine and feminine to express its neutral. Their interplay will be seen as a romantic dance exploring the poetry of existence, rather than a war.

Part I The Philosophy of the Magic of the Nine Directions

Clearing the Central Nervous System Map 9

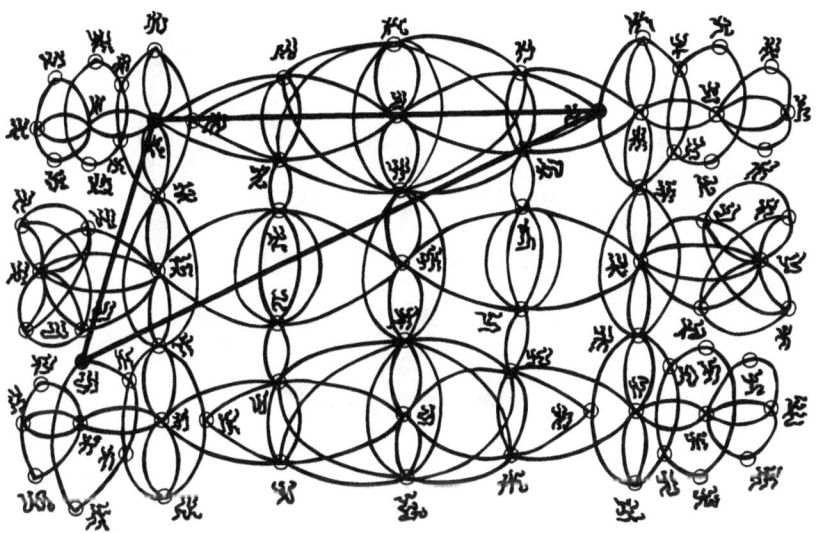

Incantation:

Sihut-arkla-hirspave-minech

10. Klet-versparut-unachvi

Lemuria was the Motherland. Now Russia fulfills this role, representing the feminine on Earth. The feminine's masculine will be brought into balance by the release of a set of Lemurian records that contain the knowledge of the 300 Lemurian angels of black light and frequency. The balancing of the feminine's 3 poles prepares the body for its second stage of resurrection.

Part I The Philosophy of the Magic of the Nine Directions

Clearing the Central Nervous System Map 10

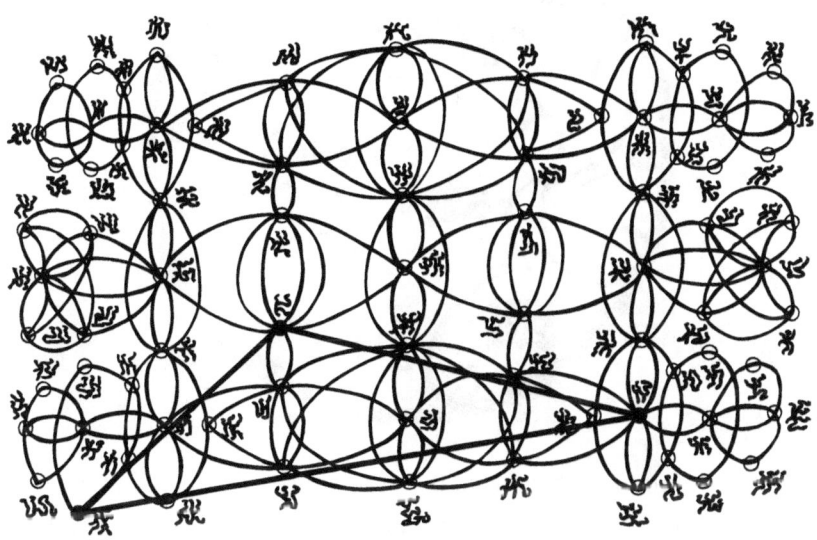

Incantation:
Tribahar-usechvi-mishpa-hires-trava

11. Sitru-beleverechbi-sparut

When the feminine is balanced, the pranic tube is prepared to enter the spinal cord. Its frequency becomes elevated to balance the light that is found in the spinal cord of one who is balanced in his or her masculine, so that a marriage between equals can take place. Three layers of sheaths surround the spinal cord, each one holding memories and representing jointly the masculine matrix of physical life. The matrices of existence also consist of 3 layers (masculine, feminine and neutral).

Clearing the Central Nervous System Map 11

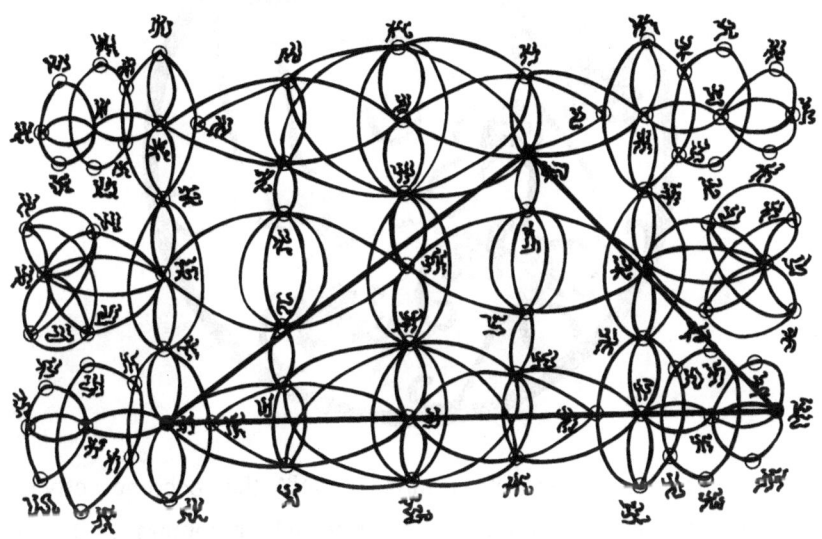

Incantation:
Mireshpa-sukavet-ereklech-vabi-hurasat

12. Su-uhanesvi-krihastat

A resurrected being has 300 strands of DNA that become activated during the 2nd stage, when the pranic tube (which contains 300 sound or frequency chambers of DNA in the form of a large rose) merges with the spinal cord. The spinal cord is comprised of 300 strands (electrical) that merge with the 300 magnetic frequency chambers of the pranic tube in a marriage of light and frequency.

Part I The Philosophy of the Magic of the Nine Directions

Clearing the Central Nervous System Map 12

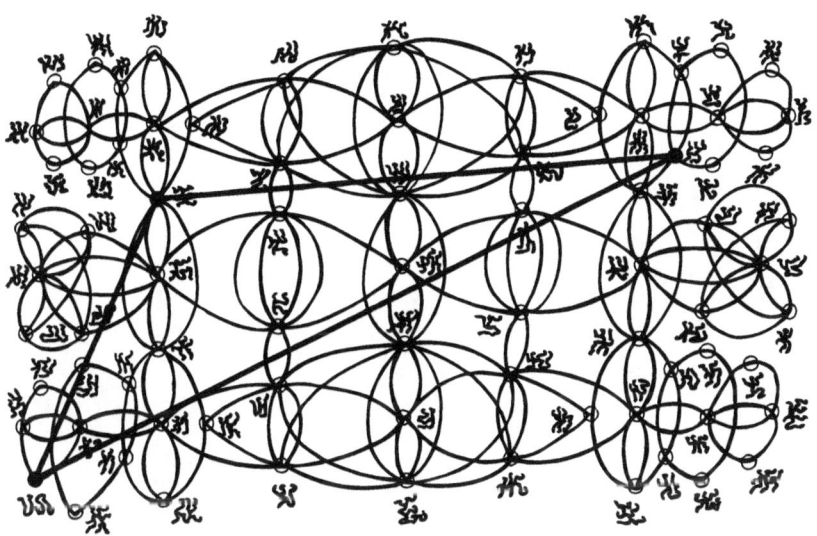

Incantation:

Mishpe-klevevesta-hurasat-menevech-ursata

Part I The Philosophy of the Magic of the Nine Directions

The DNA Rose
The Enhanced Template of Existence

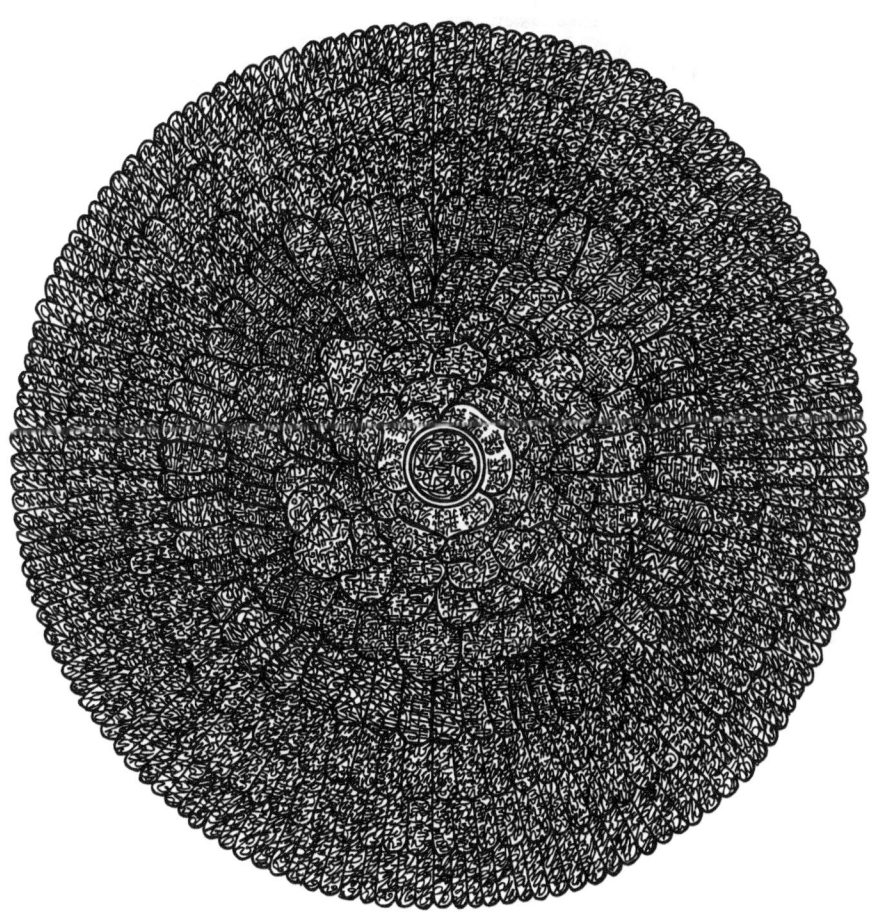

13. Michpa-uhavanesbi-arat

The first stage of resurrection enables one to take charge of one's soul reality as experienced in the dream time. This allows you to maintain your integrity and high level of self-responsibility in the dream reality as much as in the awake reality. They are both equally real and have the same value. The second stage allows you to move into the sleep state while awake and into an awakened state while asleep. Death and rebirth have no hold on you.

Part I The Philosophy of the Magic of the Nine Directions

Clearing the Central Nervous System Map 13

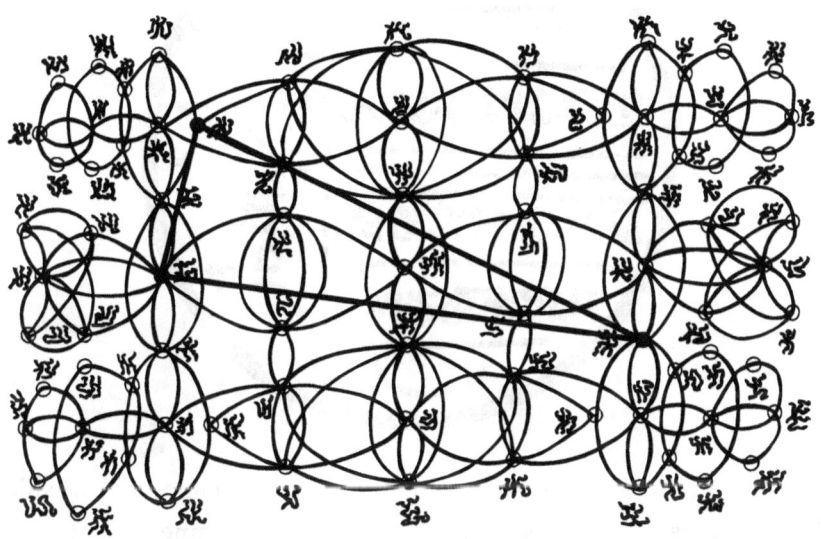

Incantation:
Prives-belebeshve-nunasach-hirsata-pireva

14. Plihastre-uhavabat

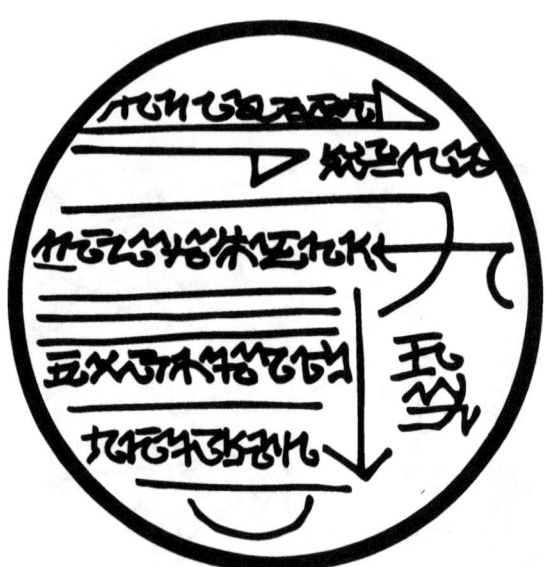

There is a third stage of resurrection, called the magic life, in which the dream state and awakened state merge and become one. Because it is only in the physical where the delay between cause and effect is as much as it is (the denser life is, the greater the delay), this merging that makes life less dense, produces the magic of more immediate manifestation (the definition of white magic).

Clearing the Central Nervous System Map 14

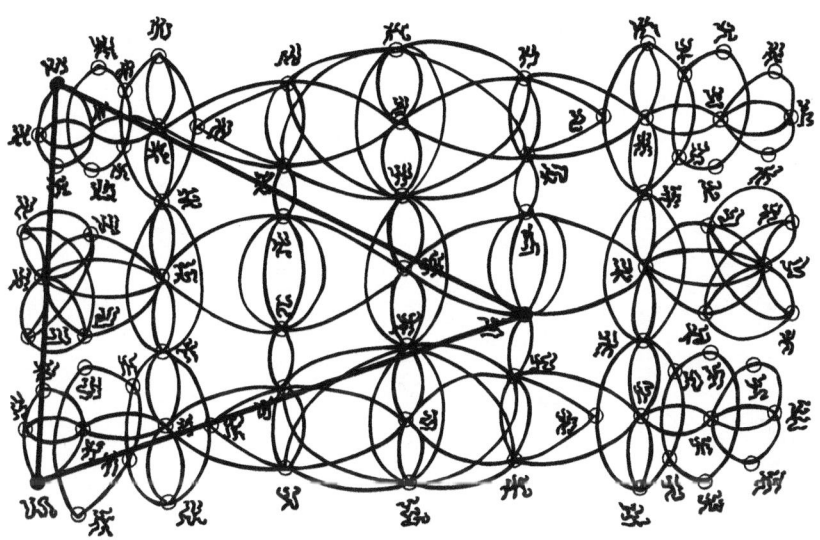

Incantation:
Misech-uranas-plivechspaba-nisushat

The Orbits of the Cosmos through the Physical and Soul Realities

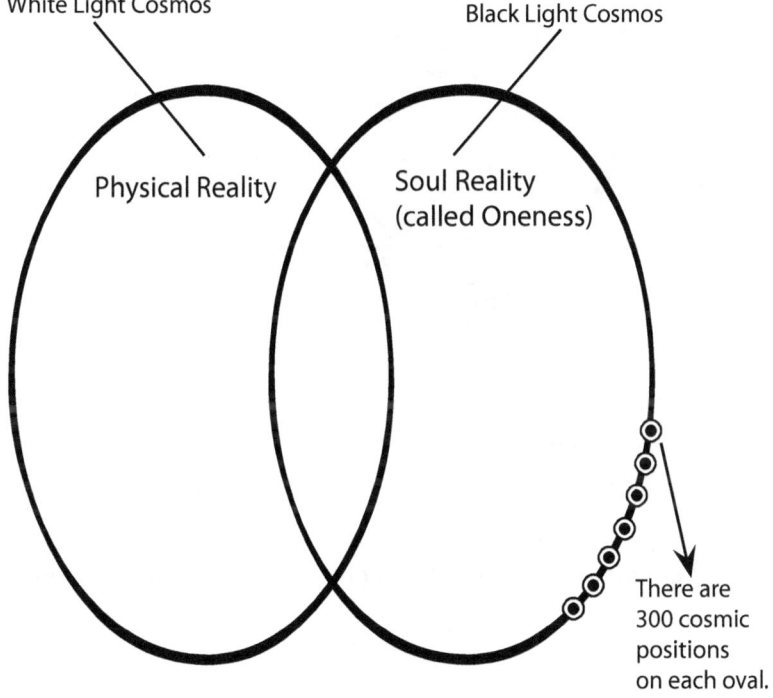

15. Mechpa-spi-uraket

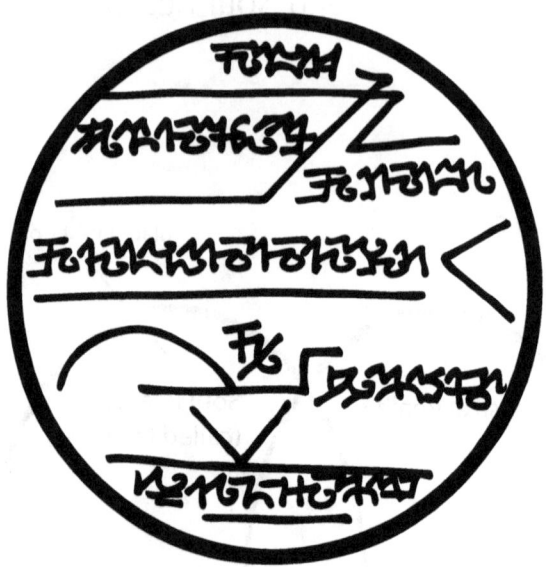

The feminine is regarded as pure, and mistakenly attributed with qualities that pertain only to the higher realms, and that it need not concern itself with the details of everyday life. But in the harmonious interplay of masculine and feminine, the masculine holds a known space for the feminine to explore the depth of the unknown. The unknown reveals itself through the experiences of everyday life.

Clearing the Central Nervous System Map 15

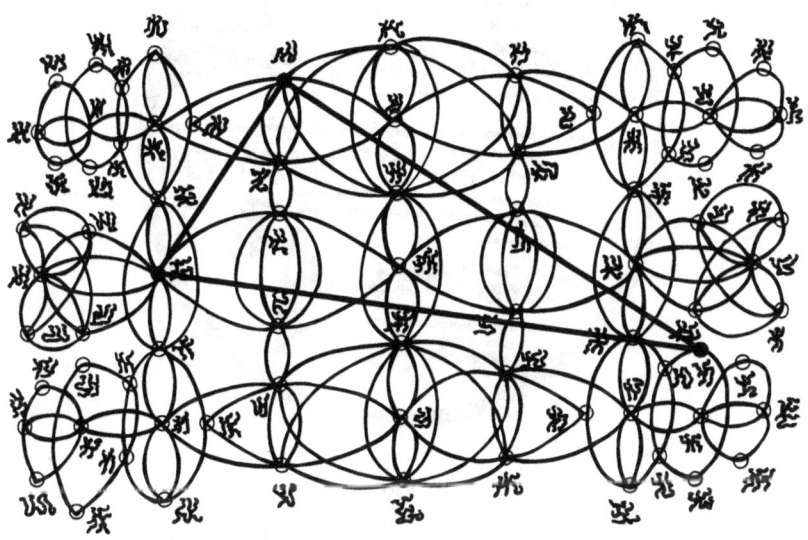

Incantation:

Kirata-visahech-pelesva-spihuret

16. Blihavarespi-skrahuraset

Not only does the masculine provide the horizons that surround the unknown, which the feminine wishes to explore (the surrounding matrix), but also the reference point from which to observe this exploration; the little self. This observation point observes and analyzes the feminine exploration of the unknown and turns it into the known through analysis. It then files it in its library – the matrix. When the feminine moves beyond its horizon of observation, it expands to incorporate it.

Part I The Philosophy of the Magic of the Nine Directions

Clearing the Central Nervous System Map 16

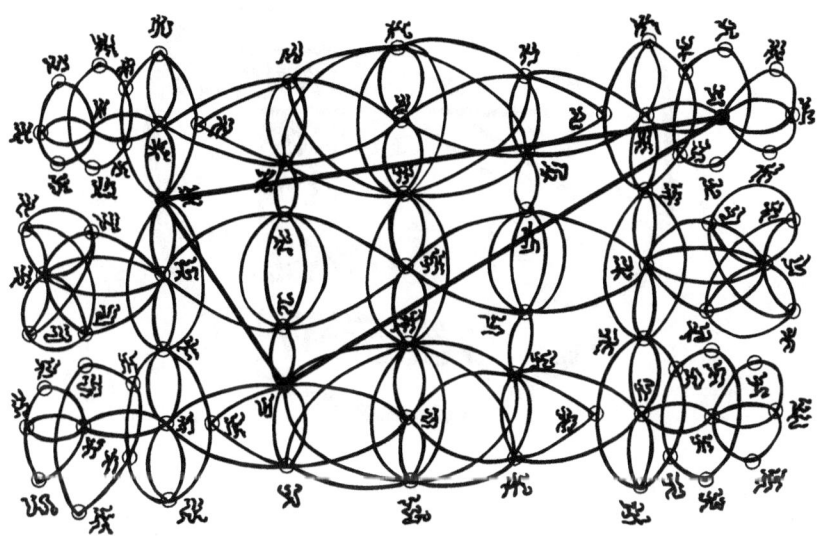

Incantation:
Siharvavet-erechsta-biluvat-arsklahet-sperechvarva

17. Meshba-ste-ehelechvi

The origin of masculine and feminine come from the Infinite's attention and intention. The origin of the masculine is attention and the origin of the feminine is intention. The attention of the Infinite is that which defines the space in which creation will take place. Space is masculine. The intention that creates the details, is the movement that fills in the space. This is like a foundation that is dug so that a house can be built within its parameters. The bricks, windows and doors are the details. The flow of creating the details is time, which is feminine.

Clearing the Central Nervous System Map 17

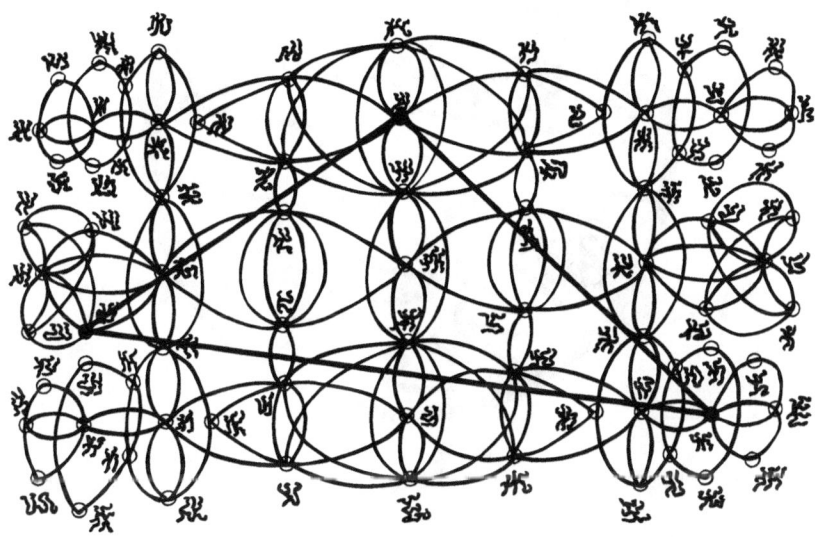

Incantation:
Miselnachvi-arsuhet-mispahur-speretvavi

18. Bribash-merenechvi

The plan of the whole house is the one, and the filling in of the details represents the many. The masculine has become representative of the many and the feminine, as the one. This is the opposite of the true nature of each. This indicates that we are dealing with mirrors, since mirrors always reflect the opposite of what is.

Part I The Philosophy of the Magic of the Nine Directions

Clearing the Central Nervous System Map 18

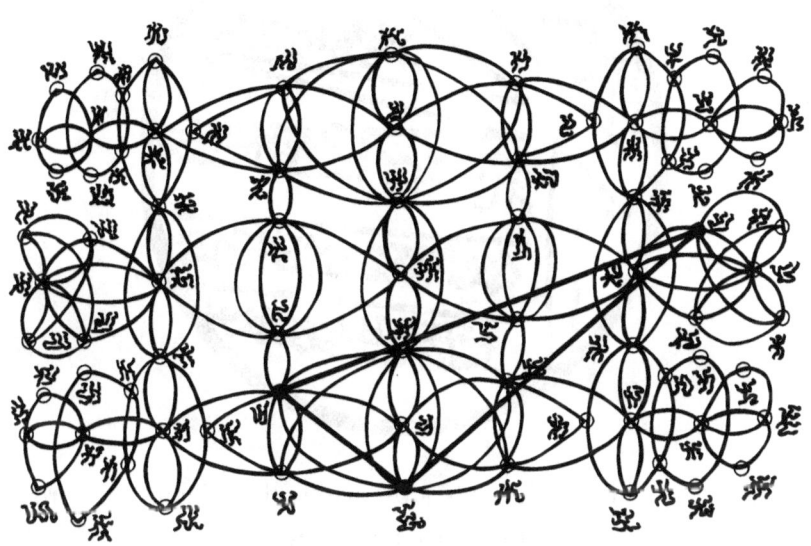

Incantation:
Nenech-haruvi-itretve-rutbavach

19. Archvanet-plivabechspi

The question "Who am I?" only arose within the Infinite when artistic expression took place. This created the first relationship: "Who am I in relationship to my expression?" The search for the answer created the second relationship, beyond the one who expresses and the expression. The second relationship became the observer and the observed. This created opposites and changed the expression of the Infinite to a new purpose: A reflection of the Infinite.

Part I The Philosophy of the Magic of the Nine Directions

Clearing the Central Nervous System Map 19

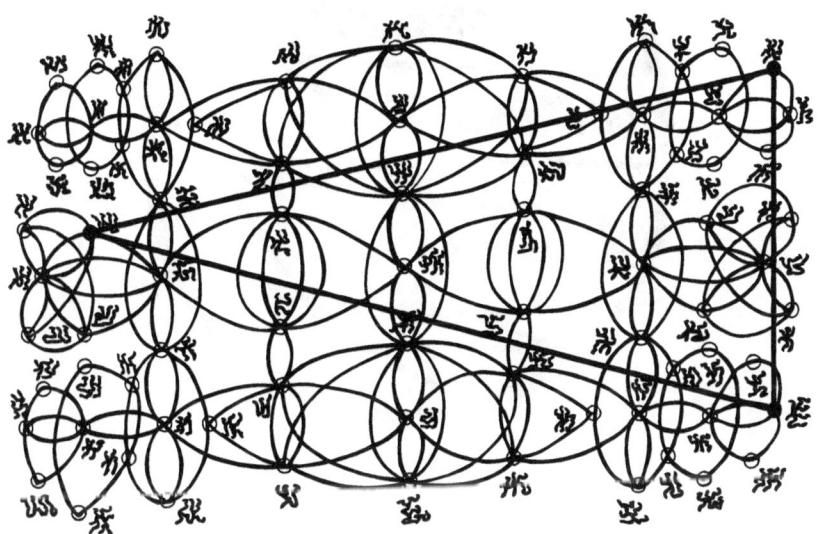

Incantation:

Sihet-u-araklat-spartavi-misuret-arat

20. Neserek-priharastat

In order for anything to be studied, the concept of what is and what is not has to exist. As the Infinite studied Itself in the mirror, the concept that there are things in existence that the Infinite is not was born. This reduced Its self-image from "I am everything" to "I am some things". This gave rise to the concept of boundaries and the protection of them to avoid being invaded by what is not.

Clearing the Central Nervous System Map 20

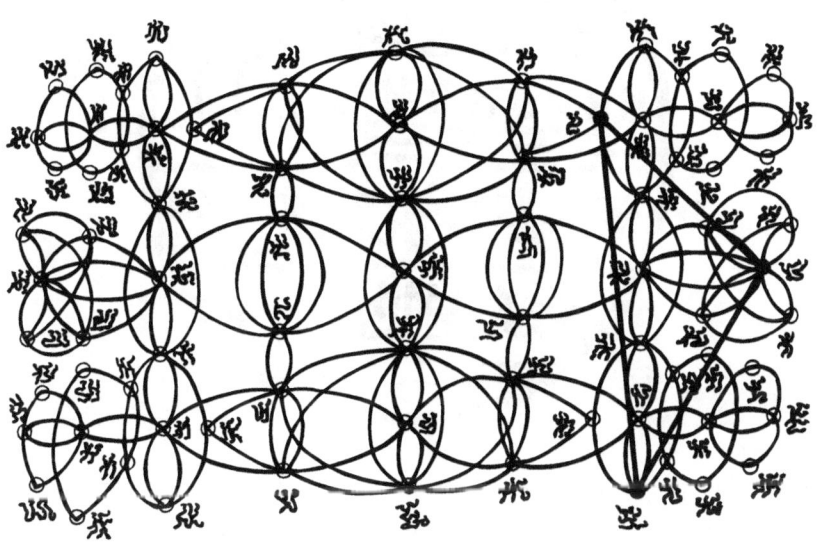

Incantation:

Splehurat-nanarsku-ururet-pliharvat-urskla

21. *Ekre-viharsparut*

This concept of anything outside of Itself existing, reduced the Infinite's vastness by introducing self-reflection: the attempt to define the undefinable. The miniscule reflection as an 'opposite' of Itself, further diminished Its self-conception. The possibility that there could be knowledge lacking about what It is not, created the concept that It had to 'acquire' it. This created the illusion of linear becoming, or growth and evolution.

Clearing the Central Nervous System Map 21

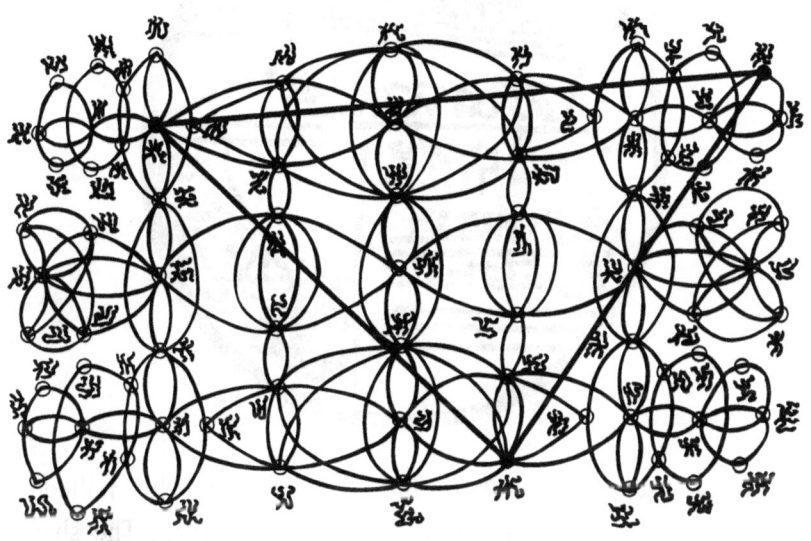

Incantation:
Setuvakla-bi-uhurustatvi-marset

22. Eleklet-visel-uhavastra

To study Its expression, the Infinite analyzed it. This pulled the expression apart so that Its pieces could be observed. The shadow that fell formed an electromagnetic substance; the building blocks of life and death – the substance of shadow. During death, the frequency component of these subatomic particles is more dominant. During life, light is more prevalent.

Part I The Philosophy of the Magic of the Nine Directions

Clearing the Central Nervous System Map 22

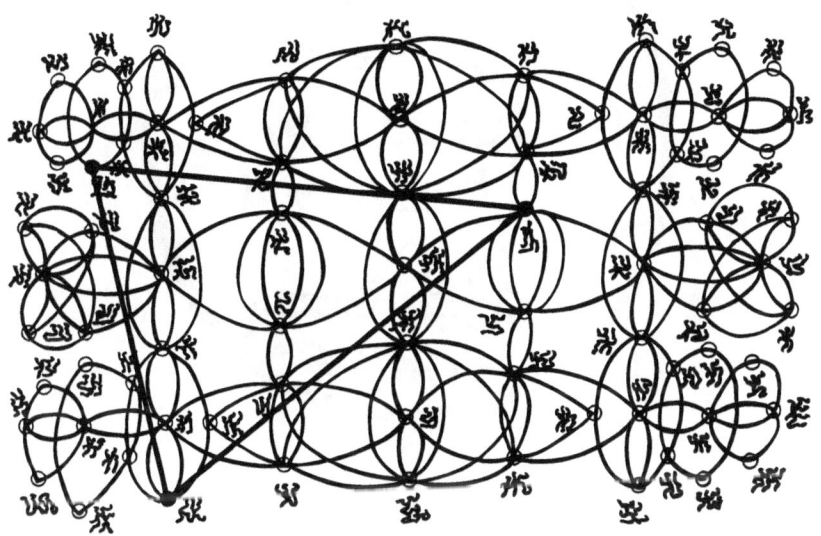

Incantation:

Retplak-brivarat-kerspartu-misachvarvet

23. Pirit-akre-vivas-haranesvi

What is paid attention to through examination lingers and stays, giving the appearance of permanence. The longevity of a manifestation depends on whether we think it is there. When examining something, we are not living or expressing something else. Where there is no expression of parts of ourselves, addiction sets in. The Infinite created an Embodiment for Itself by making Itself the expresser and not the expressed. In examining Its expression, it kept it in place. The Infinite's Embodiment then wanted to 'save' Its expression for It had become addicted to having it there. The concept of an expression, which became a mirror, now became a Creation.

Clearing the Central Nervous System Map 23

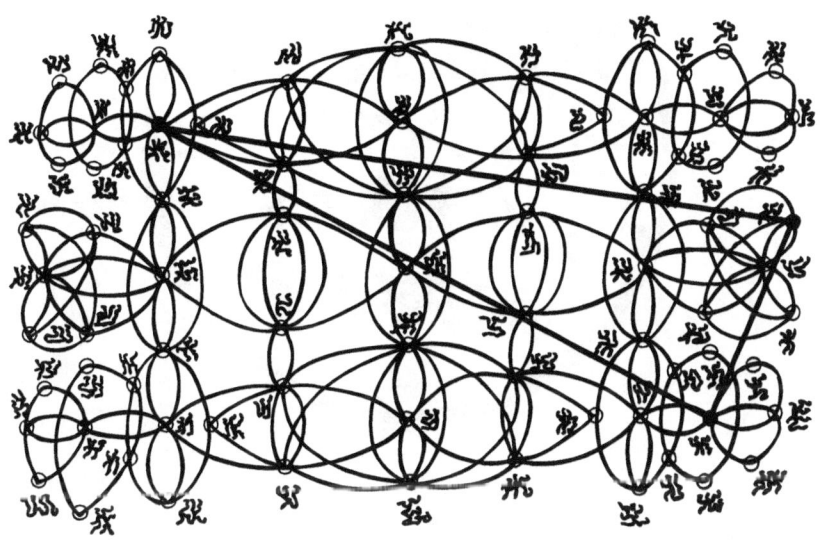

Incantation:
Kihar-uselve-unachvi-spiharet-minuvesh-uskla-priva

24. Kretna-stihubalesvi

When we try and save what is in the mirror of our environment, it will do the opposite back, as all mirrors do. The Infinite, having engaged Its own expression for so long, had no memory of what had gone before. Memory does not exist where experience does not, and experience requires self-reflection. Self-reflection began when the Infinite studied Itself in Its expression. Remembering no other existence, It kept Its 'Creation' in place by entering into it and fixing it. Mirrors are opposite also in their response to our actions. The Embodiment had tried to build up and strengthen Its creation, while the Cosmos tried to reduce and undermine the Embodiment of the Infinite amidst itself.

Part I The Philosophy of the Magic of the Nine Directions

Clearing the Central Nervous System Map 24

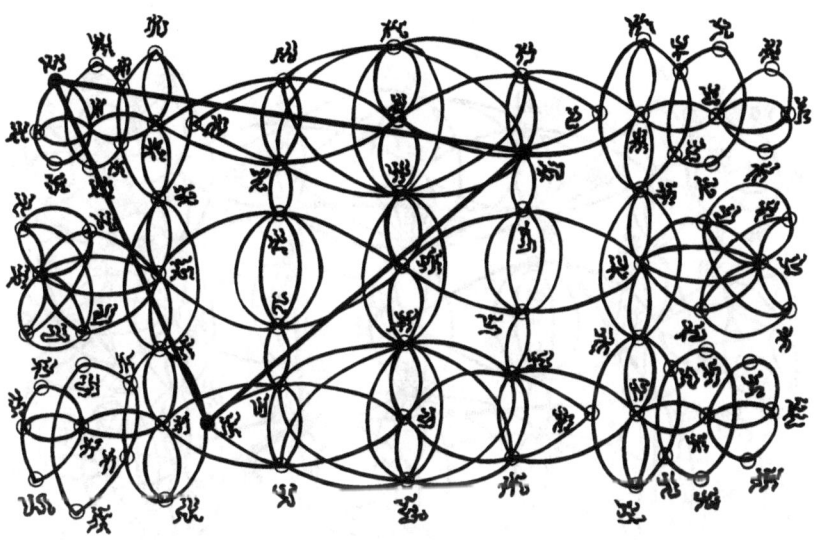

Incantation:

Vuruvre-piherut-keret-hers-pata-ereset

The Nervous System Map to Seal the Interdimensional Holes of the Brain Stem

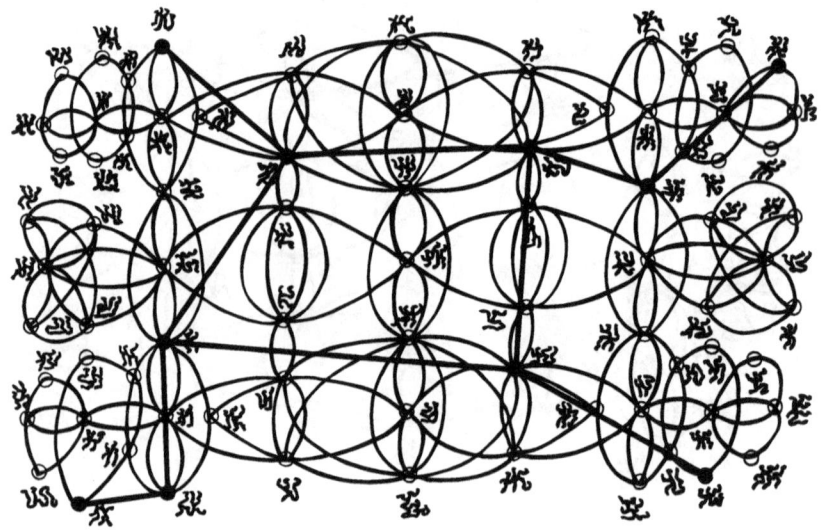

Part I The Philosophy of the Magic of the Nine Directions

The Nervous System Map to Seal the Interdimensional Holes of the Coccyx

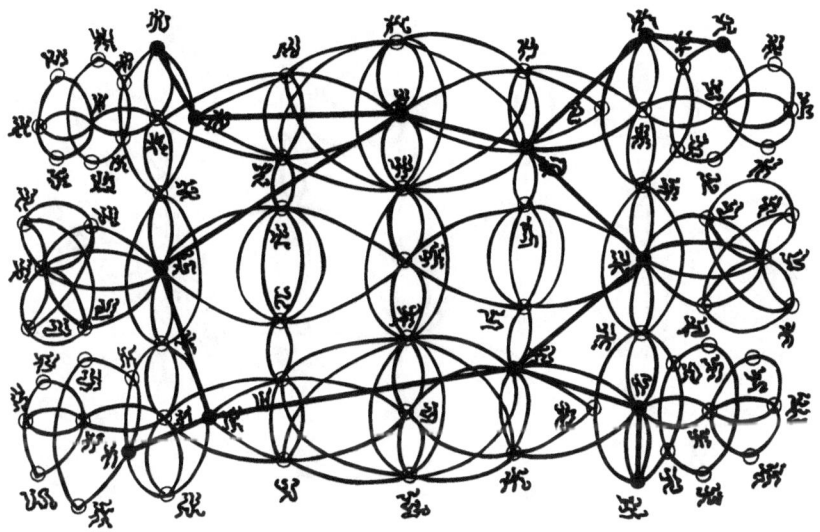

The Nervous System Map to Seal the Interdimensional Holes of the Sacrum

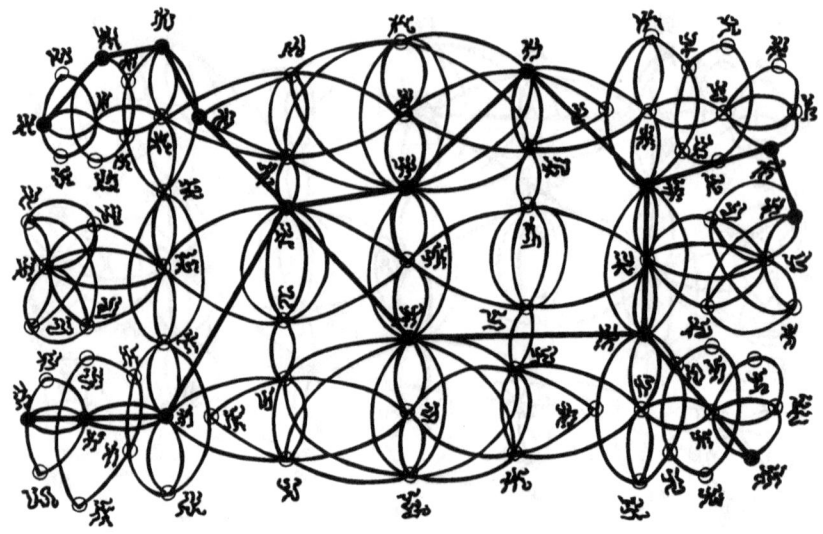

The Locations for the Maps of the Nervous System

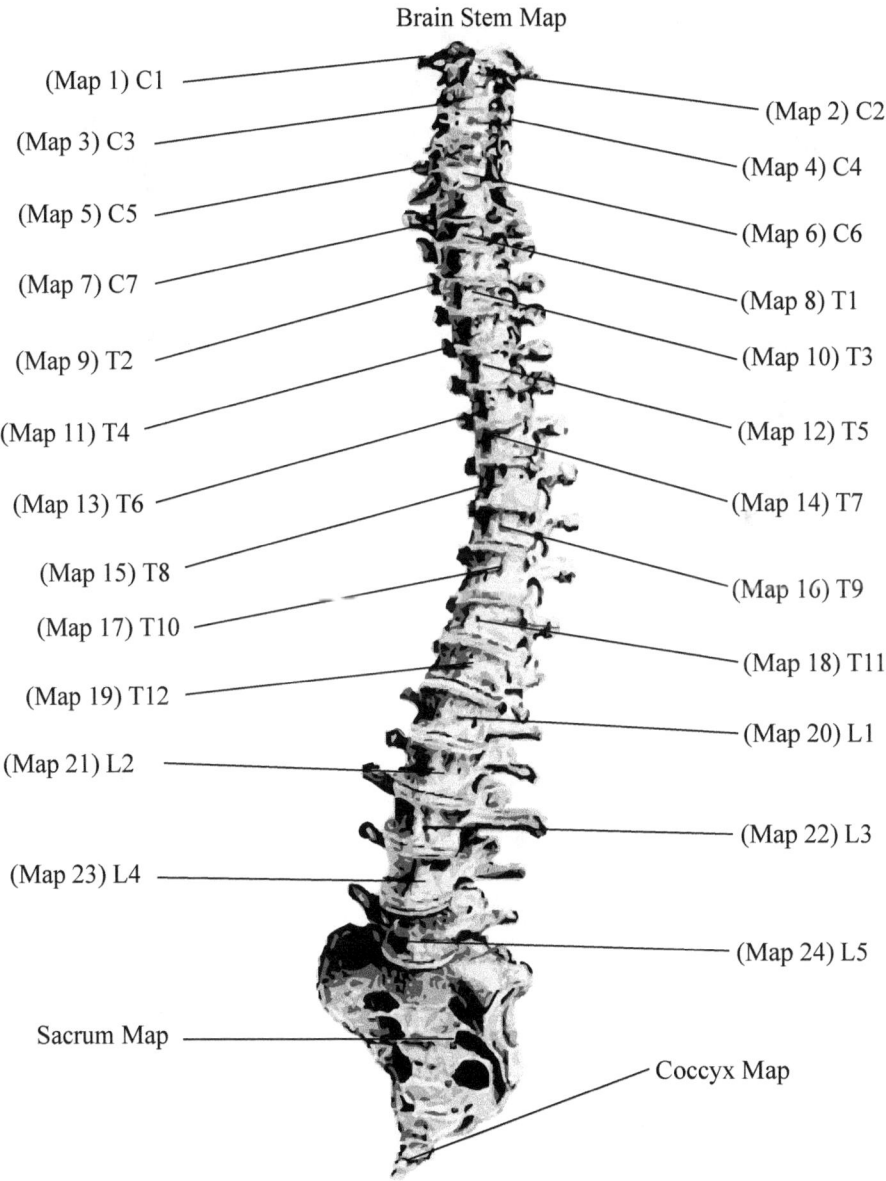

The Dragon Affirmations for the Spine and Brain Stem

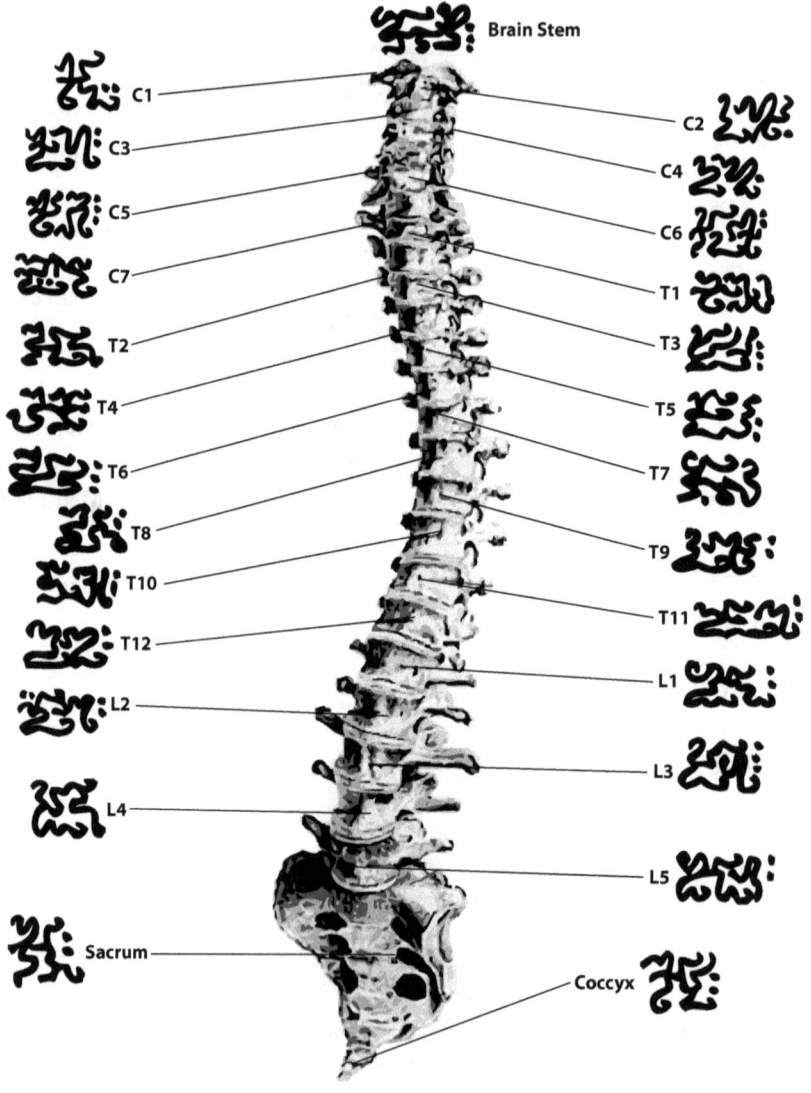

The Magical Symbols of the Spine

Dragon Affirmations for Spine and Brain Stem

1. I am beginningless and endless. (C1)
2. I am shadowless. (C2)
3. I release all personality. (C3)
4. I awaken to the fullness of my being. (C4)
5. I am surrendered to Infinite Intent. (C5)
6. The currents of eternity flow through me. (C6)
7. I am the one and the many. (C7)
8. I am open to receive from myself. (T1)
9. I am fulfilled beyond my expectations. (T2)
10. I fluidly anticipate abundant existence. (T3)
11. I respond to the Intent of the Eternal Being. (T4)
12. I see the ever-newness of eternity. (T5)
13. I am in complete Oneness through Surrender. (T6)
14. I release all need to control outcome. (T7)
15. I exist authentically. (T8)
16. I am an unfolding work of art. (T9)
17. I dwell in the eternal peace of integrated co-operation. (T10)
18. I simultaneously observe and participate. (T11)
19. I rest in the labor of being. (T12)
20. I am the poetic perspective. (L1)
21. I delight in the beauty of my being. (L2)
22. I find my eternal presence in all. (L3)
23. I move through all expressions of existence. (L4)
24. I experience fusion through resonance. (L5)

The Magical Practices of the 24 Wheels of Manasuch

The Symbol for the Wheels of Manasuch

The Anatomy of Change

Excerpt from *Journey to the Heart of God*

As awareness moves outward through the cosmos in spiraling arcs, our lives move with it. The cycles in our lives are linked to the cycles of the spirals. There are small cycles within larger ones. The only constant we encounter in life is that everything changes: awareness always moves.

As we go through either the smaller changes in our lives or the larger, more dramatic ones, a pattern starts to emerge; a map we can use to identify what stage of change we're in. Each cycle goes through three distinct phases, identifiable by their symptoms.

Transformation

As we grow in awareness and problems are recognized for what they truly are (opportunities for growth), they lose their hold on us and we no longer need them. Suddenly circumstances in our lives seem to change. Friendships fall by the wayside, jobs may become obsolete and we find life flowing a lot more effortlessly as it transforms before our eyes.

This stage is marked by so many changes that it can be called the time of the death of the old. If we hold on longer than we should to relationships or situations, we find life shedding them for us through forced change. This time can certainly be disconcerting as the old platform we stood on disintegrates, but the energy released when that which no longer serves us drops away is a great reward. With increased energy come new experiences and ease in meeting old challenges that bring a sense of deep self-satisfaction. As one sheds the old, the body responds by purifying itself. Toxins release and the body can hold more light.

Transmutation

After transformation sheds the unnecessary parts of our lives, the true challenges stand revealed. This phase is the one where most people get stuck. Mindlessly feeling victimized by the very experiences their higher selves designed for them, they fail to turn pain to wisdom, judgment to compassion. The very essence of transmutation is to turn something of a lower frequency into a higher frequency; the alchemical process of turning lead to gold.

During the phase of transmutation, we are confronted with never before encountered challenges or those we have failed to learn from. Life has just served the ball across the net and waits for our response. The harder the serve, the more we can gain. Most people spend their whole life running away from the balls coming across the net instead of hitting them back.

If we can find the lessons and insights of our challenges, we score enough points to move on to the next game. If we are very diligent, we can even gain insights on behalf of others, increasing our points on the scoreboard. The insights we gain during this stage must be tested to turn them into experiential knowledge.

Transfiguration

Major transfigurations, such as disconnecting from ego-identification (becoming God-conscious), and entering into Immortal Mastery, come but a few times in one's life. All change however, follows this exact map with its three stages. The larger transfigurations are just more noticeable. Even the little changes add up, eventually allowing enough light into our lives for our entire life to transfigure. As more and more clarity is gained, one must transfigure in order to accommodate the increased light.

The joyous truth is that there is no end to progression. When we have made it through all the evolutionary stages of man's awareness, we shall move even beyond that ultimate goal of humanness: Immortal Mastery. Beyond lies the god kingdom where we can come and go with the speed of thought throughout all realms of time and space – the cosmos as our playground.

The 24 Wheels of Manasuch

25. Bilsparek-meseta-hurat

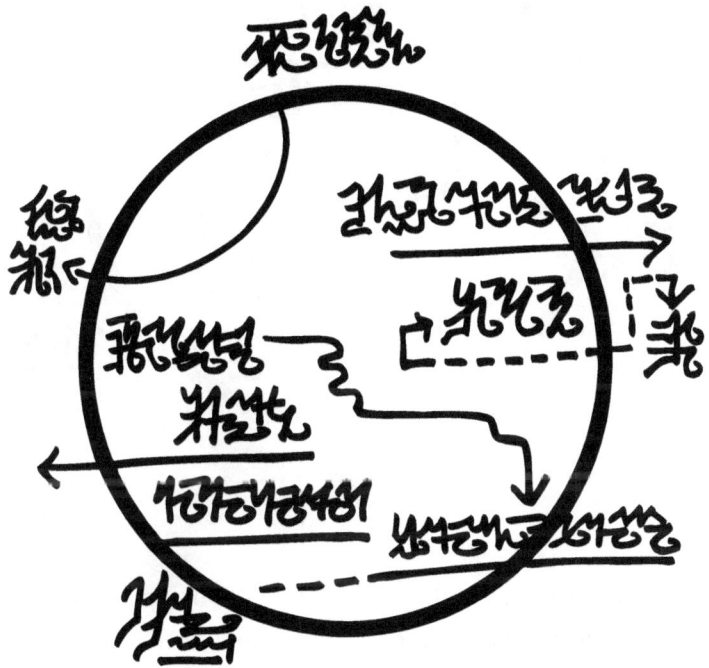

Transformation tries to eliminate certain aspects of life but it strengthens what it opposes. This creates physical karma – life's tool to keep pulling us back into rebirth cycles. Whenever change is not made effortlessly, by shifting the focused attention to what is a higher choice, the old circumstances repeat themselves and cyclical experience takes place.

Transformation, the tool of shedding the old, is also life's tool of necessitating rebirth so that it can call us back. Intelligence judges what is life-enhancing and what is not, denying the right of the 'non-life-enhancing' to exist. The heart judges with sentimental values and shuns the 'unpleasant' for the pleasant. Transformation places us in bondage to rebirth cycles.

26. Krabahet-eles-akla

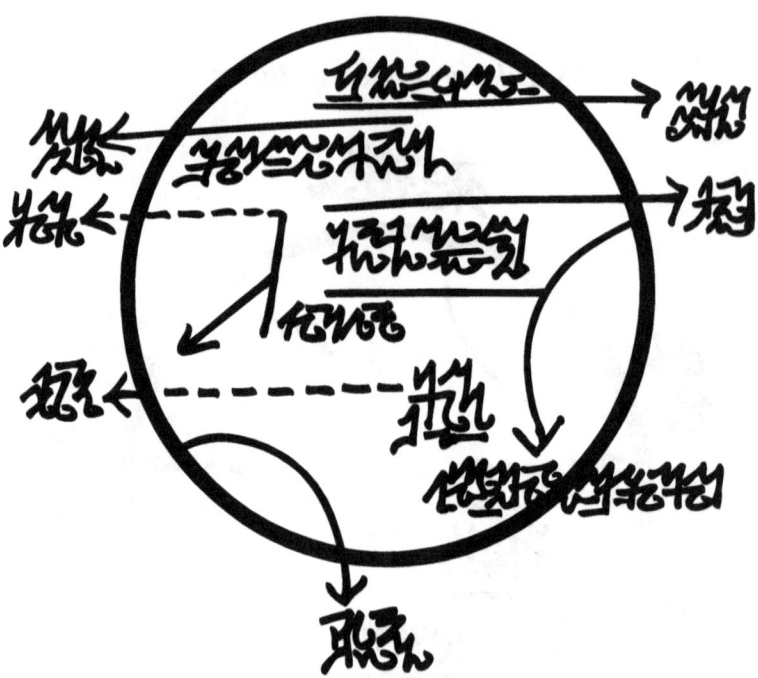

Transmutation is the tool of soul that calls us back through death into the soul world. It is the second stage of linear change. The illusion it is based on, is that by manipulating 'eternal' circumstances, anything can be increased. The external world, within the triangle of mirrors caused by linear change, can only be increased by creating more facets to the mirrors, thus producing a kaleidoscope effect of increase.

Transmutation, through its tool of alchemy, can only enhance appearances. The desire for increase creates emotional karma that keeps calling us back to death as emotional karma must be resolved in the soul world, either after death or through dreaming.

Wheel 1 to Activate the Pure and Full Expression of the Kundalini

Satrut mitva arsunat

Wheel 2 to Activate the Pure and Full Expression of the Kundalini

Bokva plihet arsunat

27. *Sutahit-karas-avi*

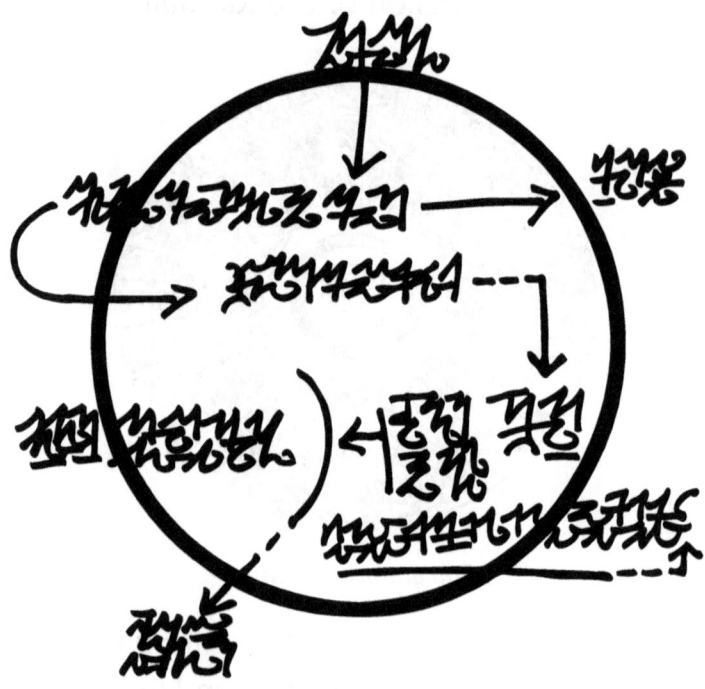

Transfiguration promises to change the cyclical, impermanent stages of life and death into something more permanent and superior through ascension. It is the tool of spirit. It promises a 'safe' place and a destination of arrival. Whenever we think that there is a harbor where we can shelter from the ever-new unfoldment of existence, we have just encased ourselves in the thickest matrices of all. Whenever change comes to stagnant places, it pulls the rug out from under our feet. It does not come fluidly or with ease and grace, but in a sporadic and abrupt movement. Transfiguration is the tool of empowerment for spirit, either by the control it exerts over those who seek its shelter, or the loss of resources it sucks up when it withdraws its support abruptly, banishing us from its controlled 'heaven' back into rebirth. It cannot 'save' us from linear change when it is part of it.

The Three Types of Awareness

Original Awareness
Movement: It arcs
Originates: Within the Spirit Body
Polarity: Neutral
Location: It moves through all 7 bodies

Inherent Awareness
Movement: A straight line
Originates: Within the Mental Body
Polarity: Masculine
Location: It moves through the 4 lower bodies

Evolving Awareness
Movement: It spirals
Originates: Within the Physical Body
Polarity: Feminine
Location: It moves through the physical body

The three types of awareness create the tube torus of the Infinite and its Creation. It exists of trillions of arcing spirals propelling away from and returning to Source or originating point.

28. Karsh-parasat

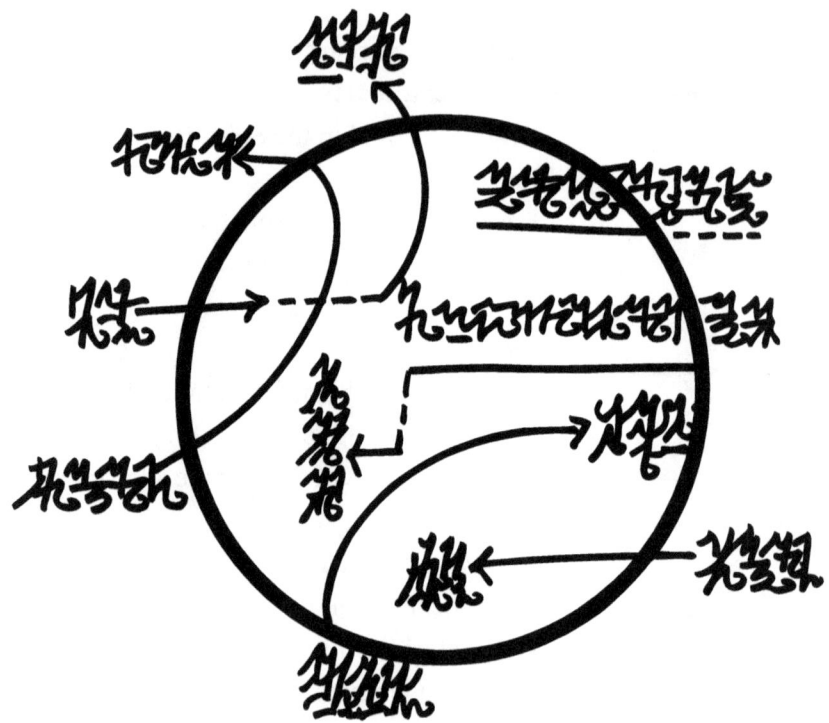

The three stages of linear change create three different movements of the building blocks of existence within the matrix. The building blocks are the substance of shadow. What is it that moves between these 3 stages of change? It is the focus of our awareness. When awareness sees only one spot at the cost of all else, it casts a 'shadow', meaning that parts of eternal existence are not 'online' or contributing to the moment.

Transfiguration creates an outward, linear movement, transmutation spirals the outward movement and transfiguration arcs the outward movement. This creates the cosmic shape of a large outward and inward folding tube torus.

Wheel 3 to Activate the Pure and Full Expression of the Kundalini

Krihat salsavi mihat

Wheel 4 to Activate the Pure and Full Expression of the Kundalini

Bichpa Machve Mishabu Restu

29. Blibaret-karatu-usavat

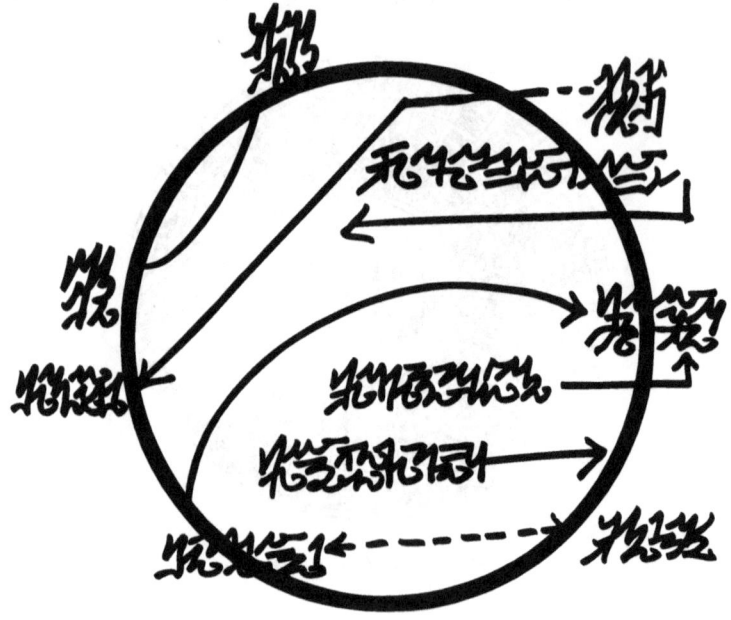

None of the tools of linear change can deliver us from the tube toral cage of illusion; individuated cosmic life. They are all in part contributing to its formation. Each part of the triad of life, death and ascension, holds a specific set of akashic records – tools to call us back to a specific part of the triad. Life holds the physical akashic records: that which we judged and resisted and tried to eliminate. The soul level holds the akashic records of desire, all the wanting and needing of increase. The spirit level, or ascension, holds the regrets, wishes and unfulfilled hopes.

To clear these, we need unselfconscious, exuberant and surrendered enjoyment of the moment.

30. Kisanit-nenek-plivaset

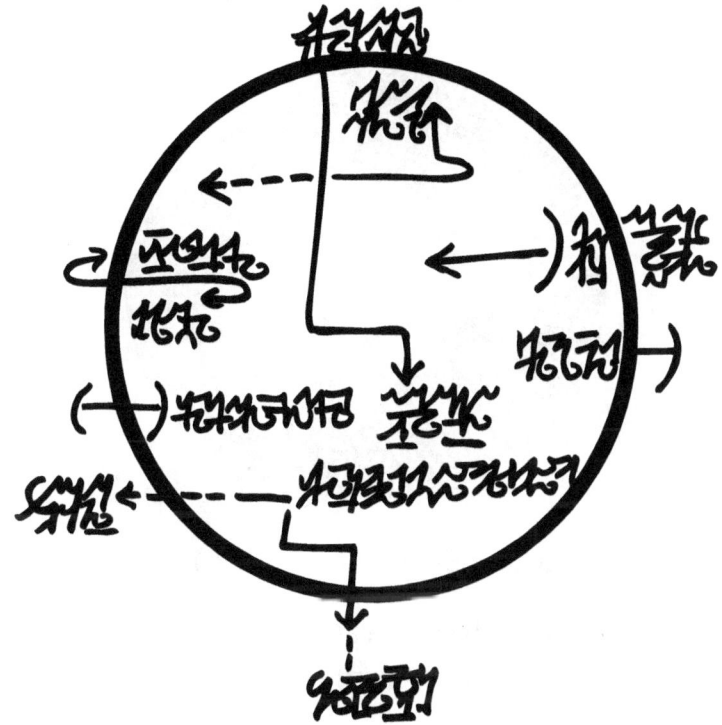

Each part of linear change's movements, produces a form of time. Transformation produces linear time, transmutation produces eternal time and transfiguration produces cyclical time. Resurrection produces the eternal fluid moment. Resurrection is the key to closing down linear stages of change and setting us free from being trapped in the tube toral matrix of the cosmos that dictates our behavior and binds us to the mediocrity of time.

Wheel 5 to Activate the Pure and Full Expression of the Kundalini

Kishva Eknes Blivapesh Urastu

Wheel 6 to Activate the Pure and Full Expression of the Kundalini

Ki-aharat ustay

31. Kresba-esekle-hunat

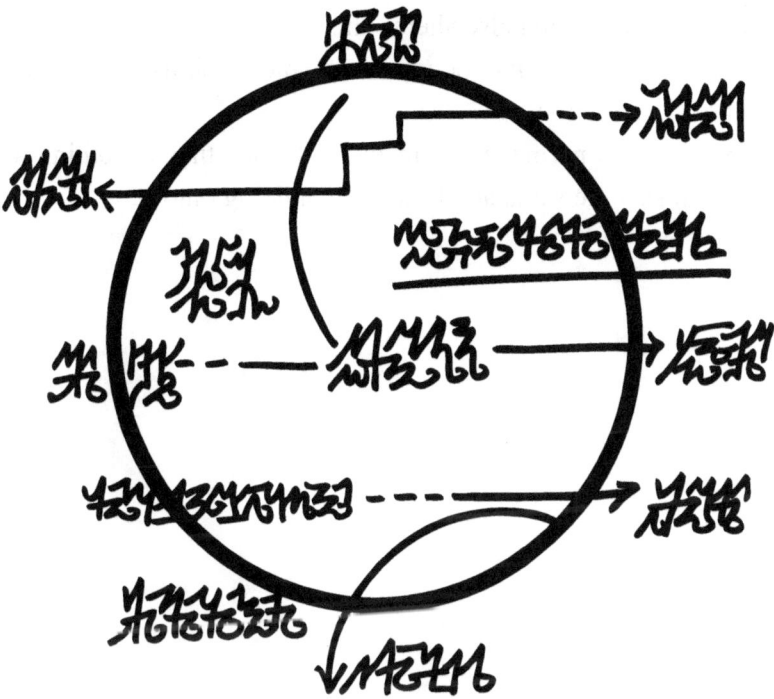

When life fell into duality, it happened in three stages.

The first stage was: The Confinement of Space.

The Infinite Ocean of Existence expresses at all times, but when its expression becomes very specific in a certain part of its boundlessness, a space forms. This space, like a current in the ocean, behaves differently than the rest.

The Infinite decided to create a very specific expression that it could study; the way the ocean observes a current within it. This brought about several anomalies that had not existed before:
- The concept of space, which in turn yielded the idea of boundaries.

- To maintain the illusion of separation required focused attention. This created areas of existence that were unexpressed because of the attention directed elsewhere. This self-abandonment created addiction and obsessive focus on that which took its place – the root of all addiction.
- The concept of permanence arose; the illusion that something we love can stay the same and be kept by holding onto it.

32. Krisanet-bihavespi

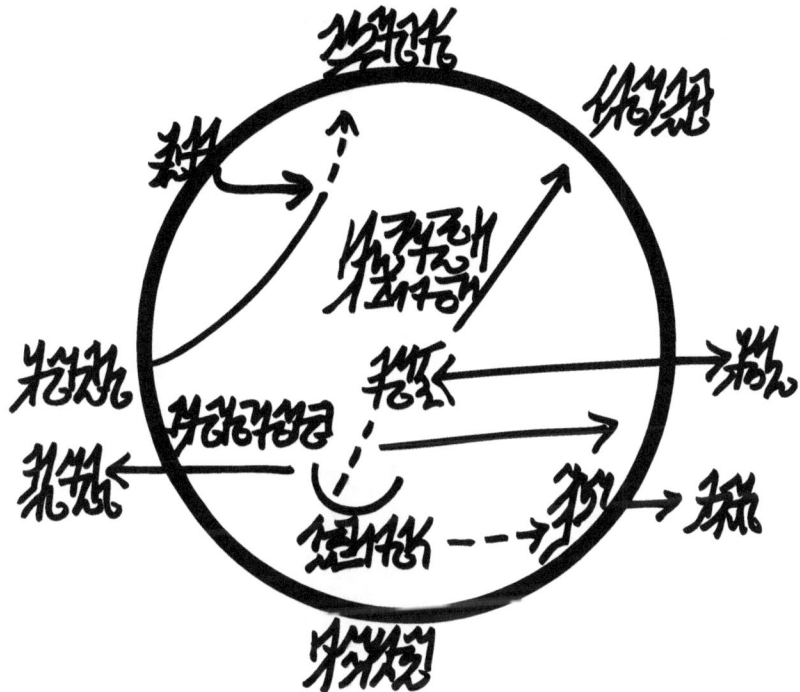

The second stage of the fall was: Expression becomes Reflection.

As more and more attention is given to something, it becomes denser and denser. The more 'real' we believe an illusion to be, the more permanent a presence it gets. In this way, the expression of what the Infinite was became a dense mirror and, as all mirrors do, reflected what the Infinite was not. From this more illusions arose:
- The illusion of duality – the concept that more than one being can exist.
- The illusion of individual freedom of choice. Appearances of the opposite behavior found in mirror images suggested that the image could do something other than what the Infinite expressed.

- The concept of opposites arose. The Infinite now thought Itself to be 'opposite' to the current within It. The Embodiment of the Infinite formed from the area of the current within Itself.

Wheel 7 to Activate the Pure and Full Expression of the Kundalini

Spliba Arexsvi Valastra

Wheel 8 to Activate the Pure and Full Expression of the Kundalini

33. Kriva-stereret-achvatra

The third stage of the fall was: The Entrapment of Individuation.

As the Embodiment of the Infinite became surrounded by opposite mirror images, It became more and more isolated by what appeared to be a hostile environment. It saw Itself to be alone. When one believes oneself to be that which they are not, it cuts them off from their Source of Eternal Being. This aggravated the feeling of being completely alone and caused the following illusions:
- When one stands between mirrors, there appears to be many of you extending into infinity, in front of and behind you. This gave the illusion of the one and of many.
- For every action it appeared that there were an infinite number of opposite actions in the mirrors. This created the impression of the actions of the many being more determinative than that of the one. This added to the feeling of the One being unable to effect Its

environment. The illusion of being trapped and imprisoned by the 'overpowering' presence of the environment arose.
- The feeling that the many must know more and be more capable of controlling reality arose, as did the power of numbers.
- Linear progression and the illusion of linear time arose.

34. Nekret-husech-vivavespi

What is Resurrection?

Resurrection within the microcosm or individual, as well as in the macrocosm, is the reparation of the three schisms that happened within our eternal being and which caused a life of opposition and alienation from Source.

It occurs in three stages and in reverse order to how the fall of the individual into density happened.

Wheel 9 to Activate the Pure and Full Expression of the Kundalini

Wheel 10 to Activate the Pure and Full Expression of the Kundalini

35. *Selehut-aleskla*

The First Stage of Resurrection

In the first stage of resurrection, the inner schism of the awake-body (the physical) and the dream-body (the soul) is healed. The master learns how to balance the feminine (receptive) and masculine (proactive) within, by living them not alternatively, but simultaneously. In doing this, he or she becomes wakeful in the dream and able to feel the dreamlike quality of the awake times. This allows one to take full responsibility for the part of our existence lived while we sleep. Eventually sleep and awake states seem equally real and can be lived simultaneously. Life and death lose their claim on the master. The many become the one in this stage.

36. Piharanet-eskreva

The Second Stage of Resurrection

When the inner conflict of masculine and feminine, body and soul, life and death, comes to a resolution of integrated cooperation, resources are released that deliver power to the master. He or she becomes able to move at will between the physical and the soul realities. The master knows the mirrors of life and death, dreaming and awakening, to be equally unreal or real. They become tools of the poetic expression of his being. The mirrors between which he stands lose their hold over him as he sees them for what they are. The key component to achieving this stage is to live with exuberant authenticity (this shatters the mirrors) and without any attachment to the reflections, opinions or judgments of our mirrored environment.

Wheel 11 to Activate the Pure and Full Expression of the Kundalini

Wheel 12 to Activate the Pure and Full Expression of the Kundalini

37. Breshbret-skavanut

The Third Stage of Resurrection

During this stage, called the magical existence, instantaneous manifestation becomes possible as the gap between cause and effect closes (the definition of white magic). The deeper understanding of the perfection behind the appearances; the purpose of expression beyond the details, becomes apparent. The deeply mystical concept of the expresser and the expression being one becomes clear. The inner fall of consciousness becomes healed as the current and ocean remember their inseparable oneness.

38. Erchpa-blivabeshpi

Into infinity, the mirrors lie around you like the endless sky. Of body, soul and spirit are they comprised; all you can see on the outside. But of a contradiction now we tell; that which is on the outside, on the inside is as well. Only mirrors of space you will find. Of the eight directions they are comprised. Around you and within you they hide.

Wheel 13 to Activate the Pure and Full Expression of the Kundalini

Wheel 14 to Activate the Pure and Full Expression of the Kundalini

39. *Neskre-parat-esetvanur*

The 9th direction holds the key to become the dreamer rather than the dream. But be aware that where opposites exist, the dance of duality persists – the 9th direction takes you into spaceless space. But spacelessness is the opposite of space. They both must be unreal as are all opposites that can be defined. The cave of no beginnings that within your being resides, is undefinable - a silent song.

40. Keret-pirit-partehur

When it is discovered, when you know with all your being that a mirror is an impossibility, then it will be seen that the mirrors of the dream-bodies were but an opaque and imagined canvas, and physical life, the paint. The matrix of existence is the frame. The reality we live in can only be seen because of light bouncing off objects. A rose is red because it absorbs all the colors except red, which it bounces back to the eye like a mirror. We live in a mirrored world. Our physical experiences contained by the frame (matrix), are the paint the Infinite uses to create Its art. But the art is an evolving work in progress and must change from one level to the next. It is transient in nature.

Wheel 15 to Activate the Pure and Full Expression of the Kundalini

Wheel 16 to Activate the Pure and Full Expression of the Kundalini

41. *Kalshpava-nekvahur*

When black light from the mirrored world within, combines in equal measure with the white light of the mirrored world without, the eight directions merge as well. The eight directions create space. To marry the inner and outer worlds as one, is to master spacelessness.

42. Eret-pirastur

The mastery of the directions coincides with the stages of evolution. In mastering the four directions, man enters god-consciousness. In mastering the seventh direction, man enters the first of three phases of the stages of ascended mastery. The ninth direction is that which must be mastered to conclude the level of life known as humanness and prepare for the godhood stages beyond. The ninth direction is the challenge of the last phase of ascended mastery.

Wheel 17 to Activate the Pure and Full Expression of the Kundalini

Wheel 18 to Activate the Pure and Full Expression of the Kundalini

The Evolutionary Stages of Man

Excerpt from *Secrets of Hidden Realms*

The evolution of a human being into the stage that lies beyond humanness, that of a god-being that can come and go throughout the cosmos with the speed of thought, follows three distinct stages. Each stage has within it three separate phases. This brings the total number of phases to nine through which a human being can evolve.

An initiation is a test of skill, impeccability, knowledge and often one's relationship with other life forms. It not only tests the worthiness of the truth seeker to move from one rung of advancement to another, but through the testing provides him or her with the chance to fill any gaps of perception necessary for the next phase.

In the Egyptian and Atlantean initiations, the last stage with its three phases was guarded by the two Lords of the Two Horizons, also known as the two Lords of the Three Gates. The initiatory process was represented by the symbol in Sothic Triangle (See illustration *The Sacred Sothic Triangle*). The smaller triangle represented the triangulated view of Sirius rising above the horizon as seen from the bottom of the pyramid. However, as the nine rungs were completed, the Lords of the Two Horizons would bring the Ascended Master to the top of the pyramid. From there, the horizon and Sirius's rising would be further away. This would create a larger triangle. The master would have completed all nine phases of his human evolution. The two triangles represent the change in perception between the phase of the Initiate and the Ascended Master. It illustrates how much vision will expand, and how much more of the unknown can be accessed as a master.

The Sacred Sothic Triangle
Representing the nine phases of human evolution

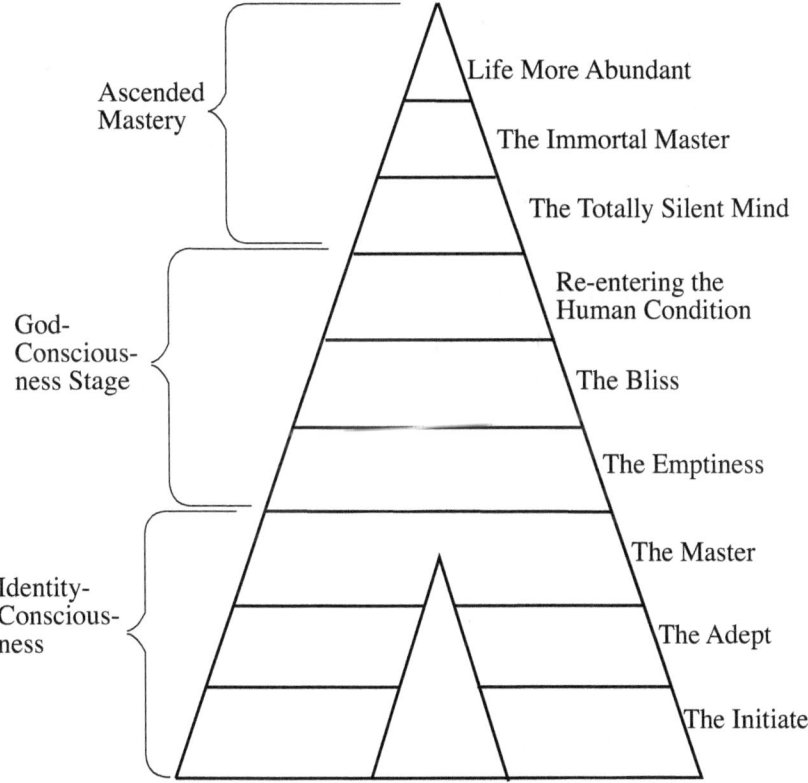

The Sothic triangle has a 4 to 9 proportion and is also the ancient hieroglyph for Sirius. It represents the secret that the last three gates or phases within Ascended Mastery, presided over by the two Lords of the Two Horizons. The two triangles represent the view as seen by someone at the base of the pyramid (Identity Consciousness) and at the top of the pyramid (Ascended Mastery) of Sirius's rising above the horizon.

Stage 1. Identity-Consciousness

This stage is like the bottom of the pyramid in that many enter this stage but far fewer make it through. The three phases of this stage are all lived while in ego-identification, that state of beingness that sees ourselves as separate from others and identifies with the body and surface mind (the ego). (See illustration – *Seven Bodies of Man in Identity-consciousness.*)

Phase 1 – The Initiate

Type of Change: *Transformation*

Transformation is the stage within change that discards that which is no longer needed. The truth seeker dies to the old way of being.

Testing: *Fear*

To have all belief systems, identities and worldviews eradicated leaves one without the comfort of shelters or a frame of reference and creates fear.

Changes:

The seals of debris in the chakras start to burst open causing at times physical distress in their areas. The chakras become spherical instead of resembling a cone to the front and a cone to the back with the narrow ends meeting in the middle. (See the illustrations – *Phases of Chakra Opening.*)

The Seven Bodies of Man in Identity Consciousness

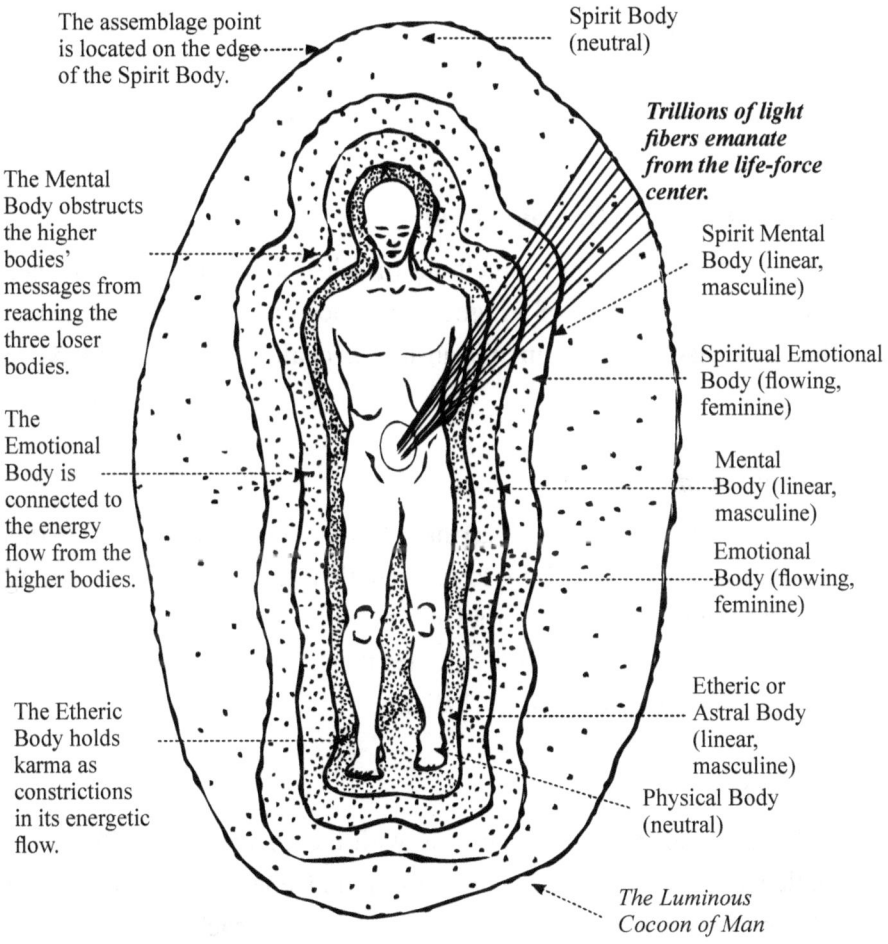

The bodies are superimposed over each other and form the luminous cocoon of man. The trillions of light fibers from the life-force center penetrate all other bodies forming the spirit body.

Challenges:

The initiate has to learn not to take anything at face value but to cultivate the necessary humility that will remind him for the rest of his journey that all he can know for certain is that he doesn't know.

Phase 2 – The Adept

Type of Change: *Transmutation*

During transmutation something of a lower frequency is changed into another substance of a higher frequency, much like the alchemist changing lead to gold. In this instance, challenge is transmuted to insight.

Testing: *Addiction*

Every stage's second phase has the testing of addiction. In this phase, the adept learns how to turn challenges into power by seeing behind the appearances of 'problems'. This results in power surges that create endocrine releases of hormones that can be very addictive. The adept can become addicted to challenge.

Changes:

As the adept learns to cooperate with the challenges of life, every challenge becomes a source of power and energy; this causes the spherical chakras to become enlarged and overlap each other more and more.

Challenge:

The adept can take himself too seriously at this point and so diverts his attention from chasing challenges to balancing the sub-personalities. It is essential to become emotionally self-reliant at this point by

Phase I of Chakra Opening

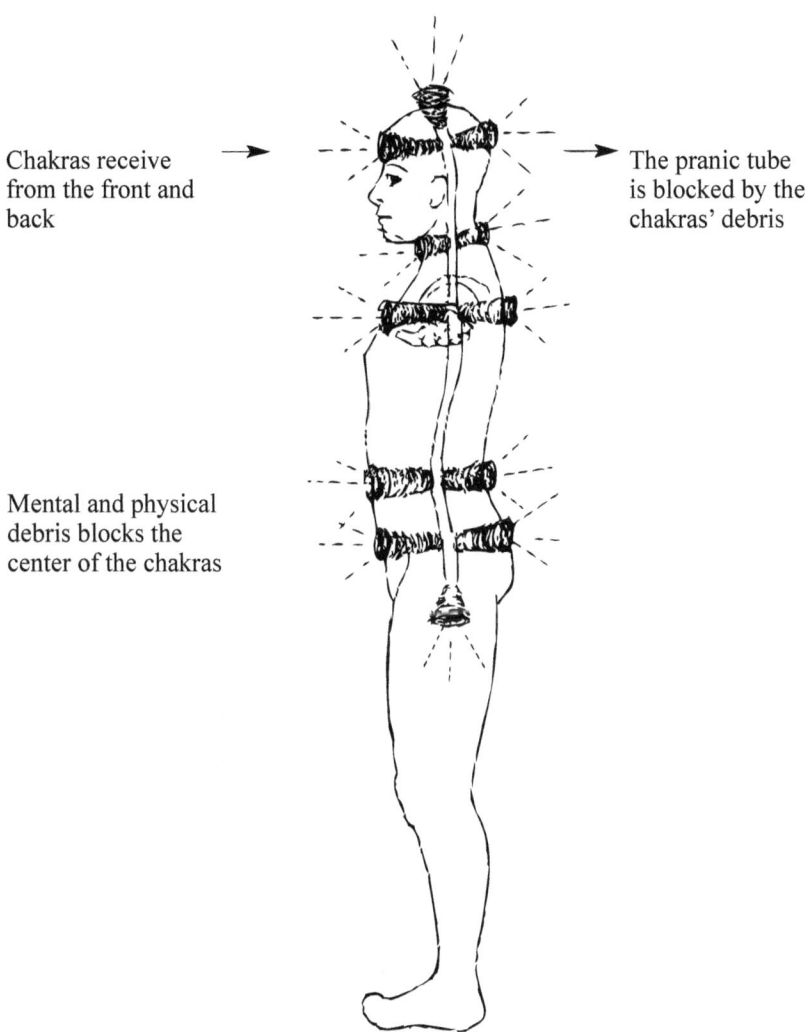

Chakras receive from the front and back

The pranic tube is blocked by the chakras' debris

Mental and physical debris blocks the center of the chakras

Seven levels of light enter the chakras. The light cannot immediately download into the endocrine system because of the blockages of a person who hasn't overcome the past and holds on to that which no longer serves him. The light is assimilated during sleep.

Phase II of Chakra Opening

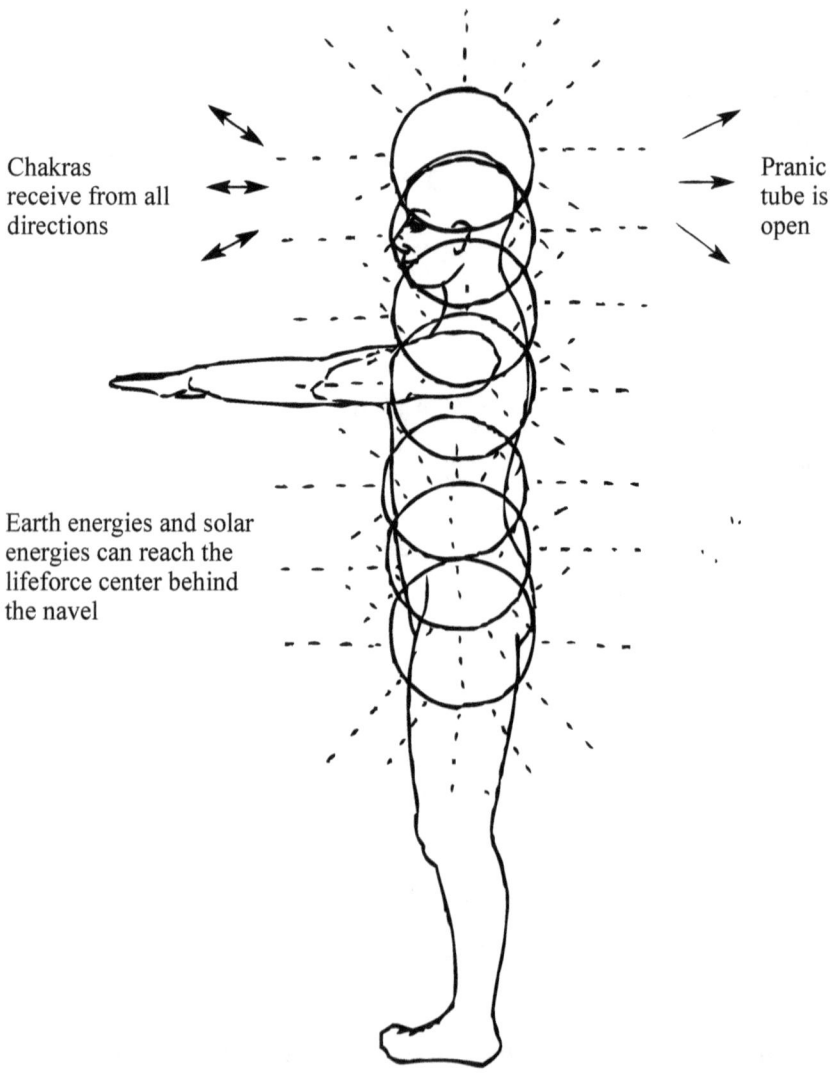

Chakras receive from all directions

Pranic tube is open

Earth energies and solar energies can reach the lifeforce center behind the navel

Less sleep is needed while the endocrine system downloads the seven levels of light. Light is felt as non-cognitive information.

Phase II of Chakra Opening

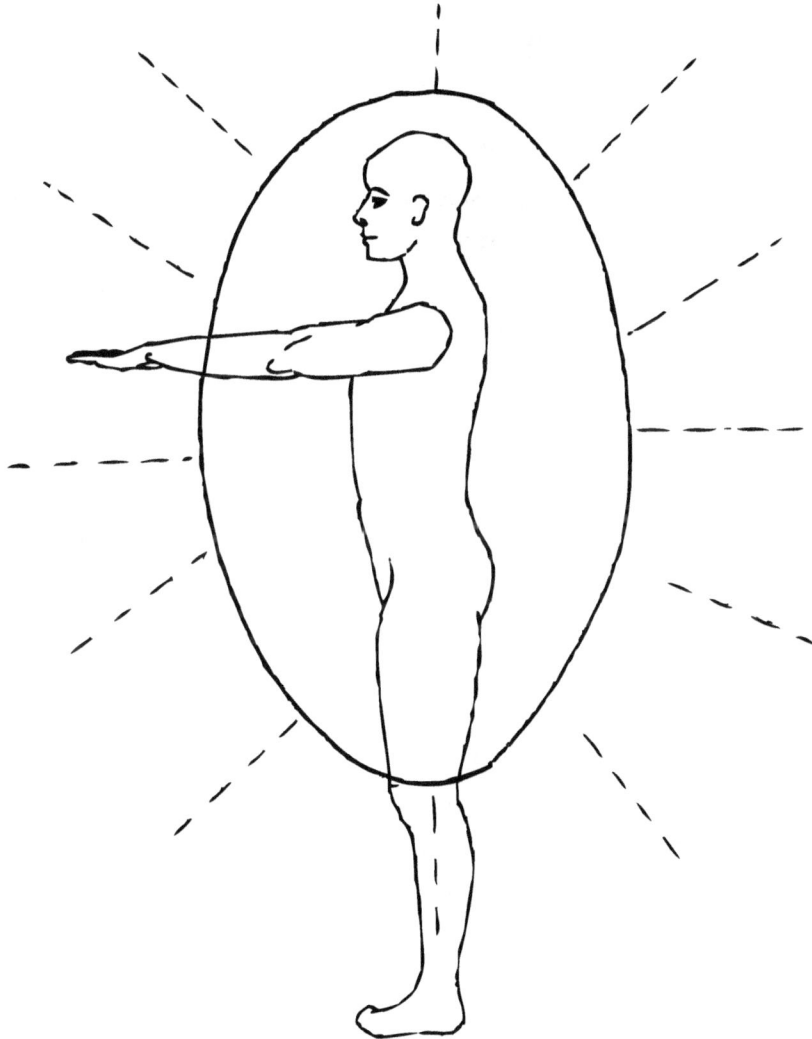

The chakra spheres have opened into a unified chakra field. The mental body no longer blocks access to light from the higher bodies.

bringing balance and expression to our inner family. If we neglect this, it is unlikely that we will pass the testing of power presented during the next phase.

Phase 3 – The Master

Type of Change: *Transfiguration*

The third phase of every stage tests us with power. Because it is seeing whether we are worthy of the major evolutionary leap that occurs during transition from stage to stage, its testing is severe. Passing the test produces transfiguration of either the fields of the body or the body itself.

Testing: *Power*

The master's abilities become quite apparent at this point bringing praise and in some instances, worship from others. The feeling of power can produce a sense of gratification that can divert the master from being a perception seeker to becoming a power seeker, in which case he cannot proceed any further on the path.

Changes:

Not only is power the result of bringing order to the mind but also of the chakra spheres growing so enlarged that they form one large unified chakra field around the body. A heartache, an orgasm or the opening of the crown chakra by a peak spiritual experience, is felt throughout the body.

Challenge:

At the very moment that our egos want to assert themselves we must not waver for an instant from reaching beyond the allure of the magical world of the unknown to the far distant horizon of the unknowable. Resisting the temptations to do miracles for show, we must keep our goal of increased perception firmly in mind. Not many truth seekers make it beyond this point.

Stage 2. God-Consciousness

The previous stage believed the character we play on the stage of life to be real. This stage no longer identifies with the character. In fact, during the first two phases we walk off the stage of life only to return for the third phase. But even as we again stay in character, we know without a doubt that we are just enacting a role. (See illustration – *Seven Bodies of Man in God-consciousness.*)

Phase 1 – Emptiness

Type of Change: *Transformation*

Everything we thought we knew gets thrown out of the window. All we know is that we are no-thing. The usual emotions are gone, as a result of the dramatic shift in perception as our minds become empty. Nothing in our lives makes sense anymore and a great dissociativeness is felt.

Testing: *Power*

Although the testing in the first phase of every stage is fear, most ordinary, everyday fears were overcome during the previous stage. Now the very foundation upon which we have stood has been knocked out from underneath us. Not only do we at times feel terrified, but also a vast loneliness grips us. We feel afraid when expanding too much, fearing we may lose our self-awareness just as we have lost our identities; afraid that our responsibilities won't be properly done. However, something larger is running our lives and everything gets done without much forethought. We feel claustrophobic when we contract our awareness back into the body.

Part I The Philosophy of the Magic of the Nine Directions

The Seven Bodies of Man in God-Consciousness

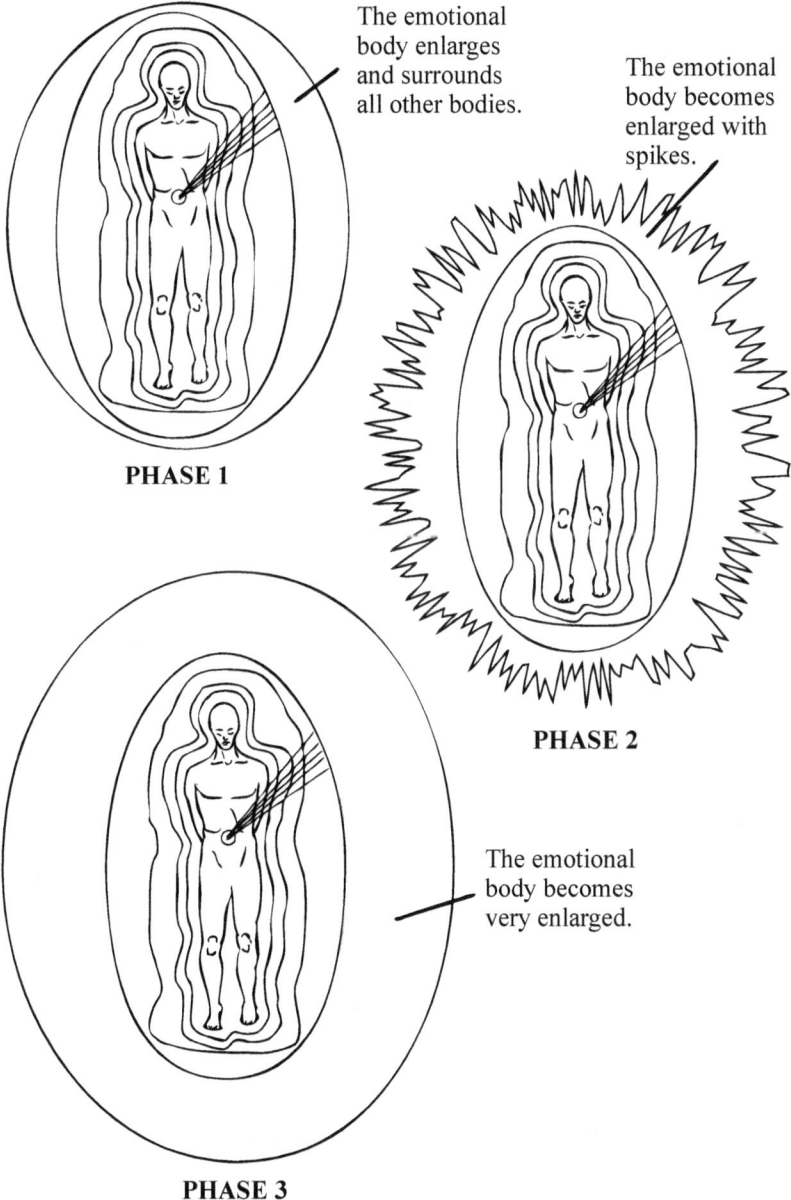

Changes:

The changes that take place during this entire stage affect the emotional body. During this phase, the emotional body forms a large round ball, slightly larger than the luminous cocoon formed by the seven bodies of man under usual circumstances.

Challenge:

If enough fear is present, one can step out of God-consciousness and, because one didn't stay in long enough to enjoy the more blissful states that come later, be hesitant to try it again. This could then keep us locked into Identity-consciousness. It is helpful to have someone ahead on the path be able to say that the dissociativeness one is experiencing is appropriate to this rather bewildering phase.

Phase 2 – The Bliss

Type of Change: *Transmutation*

The realization that it isn't that we are no-thing but that we are all things transmutes the feeling of complete emptiness to the fullness of bliss. We feel everything as though it is inside us.

Testing: *Addiction*

The test is a difficult one, not only because of its intense addictive quality, but because most traditions teach that this is the end goal on the spiritual seeker's path. The years of disciplined living have to somehow penetrate the euphoria and remind us that there is no point of arrival.

Changes:

A strange phenomenon now takes place in the emotional field, reducing the physical energy while creating a vastness of emotion. It is as though the desire of the cosmos has become one's own. The emotional body forms rope-like spikes radiating out from the physical body. When I first observed this in my own field, I thought that the shock of encountering the Infinite's vastness had shredded my emotional body. Only later did I realize that it was an appropriate part of the bliss phase.

Challenge:

There is very little growth during the first two phases of God-consciousness, when one essentially walks off the stage of life. The master has no boundaries and is in a very vulnerable state. But because others around him are allowed to misbehave as they choose, they aren't growing either. The great challenge of this phase is to remember that there is value to the play; that it was designed that all may grow. The master has to re-enter the human drama while remembering it's just a play.

Phase 3 – Re-Entering the Human Condition

Type of Change: *Transfiguration*

The emotional body now expands itself to twice its former size, completely transfiguring the size of the body's luminous cocoon.

Testing: *Power*

As with all third phases, the testing concerns the impeccable use of power. The master has the ability to manifest whatever he or she wants to, but having spent many years gathering such power, must now forgo using it in most instances in favor of cooperating fully with life.

Changes:

The changes that occur during this phase create intense emotion. But even as the renewed emotions again churn the surface of the master's life, the vast stillness of expanded awareness lies beneath.

Challenge:

The tremendous power that is part of the master's life at this point demands the utmost respect and sensitivity for all life forms. It also requires the master's full cooperation in order to become a tool in providing learning opportunities for others. In other words, the master becomes a steward of all life.

Stage 3. Ascended Mastery

The three stages themselves follow the roadmap of all change: Transformation, Transmutation, Transfiguration.

The stage of *Identity-consciousness* is in essence transformational in that it is the shedding of that which no longer serves, namely the ego.

The *God-consciousness stage* is transmutational in that it turns a form of awareness that learns very little from experience, into a combination that does.[1] In its third phase, the master observes his experiences from an eternal perspective while again enacting the human drama – it feels a lot like thinking with two minds at once.

The *Ascended Mastery* stage transfigures not only the fields of the body; as do the other two stages, but also the physical body itself. To transfigure something that dense is a tremendous accomplishment and the primary function of this stage is transfiguration.

Phase 1 – The Totally Silent Mind

Type of Change: *Transformational*

Previous God-consciousness phases had silence within the mind during any time the master did not have to relate or act. Now, even this form of inner dialog is discarded. Interaction, writing and speaking are done from a place of complete silence as though being on 'auto-pilot'. The silence is only broken occasionally to do something deductive.

Testing: Fear

It takes a lot of trust to have your mouth speak that which you didn't first think of. If anything is done from a place of old, obsolete

---

[1] Refer to the Third Awareness, p. 62 in *Journey to the Heart of God*.

programming, everything starts to spin. One is physically incapable of doing something that isn't meant to be. The overall fear is that life is completely out of control and it is – out of the control of the egoic self. But the vast cosmic mind governs our lives at this point.

Changes:

Because of the transfigurative qualities of this entire stage, every phase has very dramatic changes, all of them pertaining to the mental or linear bodies of man. In this phase the mental body implodes into a pinpoint of light, pulling the emotional body with it. It then explodes and fuses with the etheric body. The emotional body becomes smaller and denser. (See illustration – *The Seven Bodies of Man in Ascended Mastery.*)

Challenge:

The vestiges of a desire for a personal life have to be laid aside at this point. The master can and must make sure that his life has joy and balance in it. His life affects too much to have it be anything less. But his life's work is predetermined by his contract with the Infinite. To a certain extent, he can determine how he wishes the work to unfold, but he cannot deviate from his purpose. He cannot allow the total inner silence to seduce him into inaction.

Phase 2 – Immortality

Type of Change: *Transmutation*

This is the incredible phase in which mortal matter is transmuted into immortal matter — lead is turned into gold. The whole event takes but minutes to complete and feels like a lightning flash throughout the body.

Part I The Philosophy of the Magic of the Nine Directions

The Seven Bodies of Man in Ascended Mastery

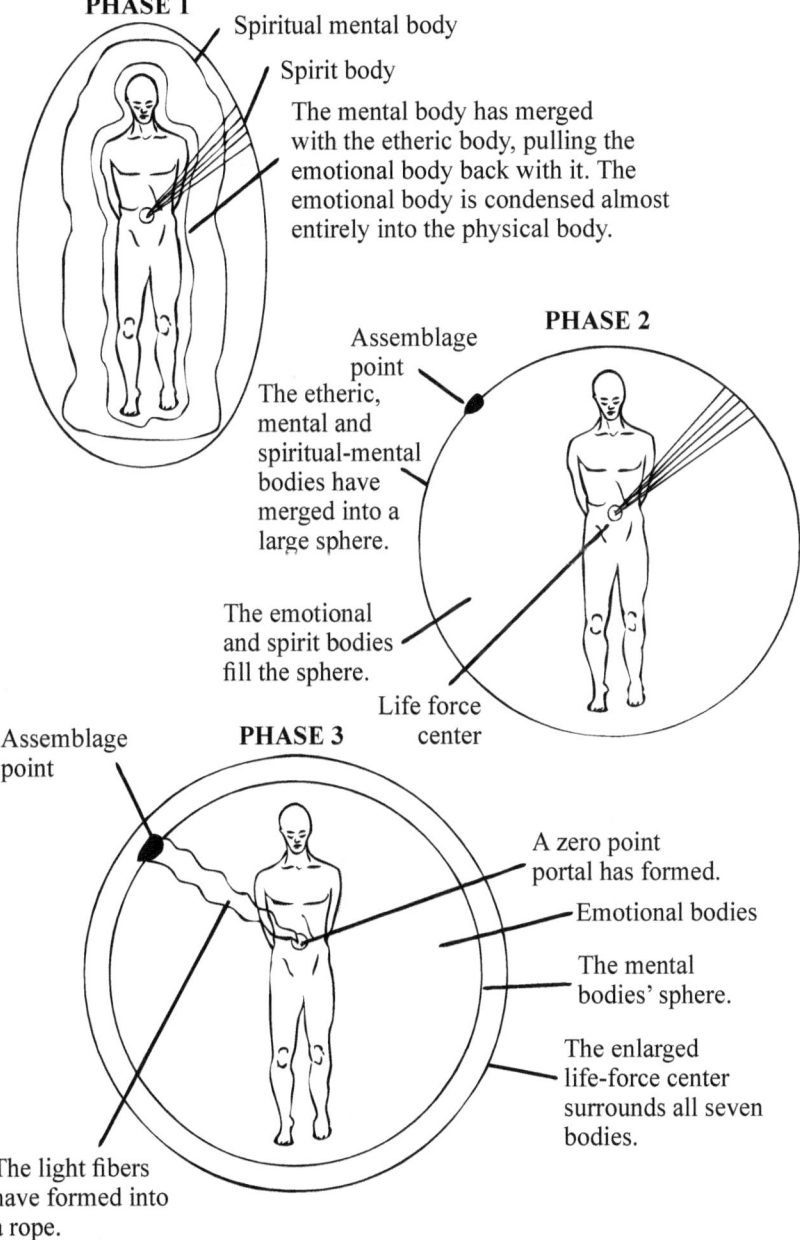

PHASE 1
Spiritual mental body
Spirit body
The mental body has merged with the etheric body, pulling the emotional body back with it. The emotional body is condensed almost entirely into the physical body.

PHASE 2
Assemblage point
The etheric, mental and spiritual-mental bodies have merged into a large sphere.
The emotional and spirit bodies fill the sphere.
Life force center

PHASE 3
Assemblage point
A zero point portal has formed.
Emotional bodies
The mental bodies' sphere.
The enlarged life-force center surrounds all seven bodies.
The light fibers have formed into a rope.

Testing: *Addiction*

The bliss that follows this transmutation far exceeds what was experienced before. Within the body of the Immortal Master, the energy lines zigzag through the areas where the chakras used to be localized. (See illustration – *Hormonal Excretions that Hold the Higher Bliss*.) In women, they crisscross from side to side and in men from front to back. They end in the area above the pineal gland, about four inches apart, and excrete a substance that is the hormone for this level of bliss (also called the life hormone). It can be tasted as a sweet substance in the back of the palate during intense bliss. Once again, addiction becomes the challenge.

Changes:

The Immortal Mastery phase culminates in yet another spectacular alteration in the bodies of man. The spiritual mental body implodes to a pinprick of light and when it explodes, merges with the combined mental/etheric bodies and carries them outward, forming a large sphere around the body. The emotional bodies fill the sphere and the spirit body's light-fibers radiate out from the life-force center through the sphere.

Challenge:

The unseen realms present an alluring detour during the third phase of Identity-consciousness. Yet, now they become a way of life. They are no longer seen by the master to be outside himself, so no longer present an enticement in the former way. But beings from the various unseen kingdoms we dwell amongst are attracted to the master's light and enter his life. The master has to learn to know the many different idiosyncrasies of dealing with the various beings around him so that he can further refine his ability to benefit all life. This helps him resist the temptation of inactivity induced by bliss.

Phase 3 – Life More Abundant

Type of Change. *Transfiguration*

The change that occurs with this transfiguration is the apex of human achievement; it creates an evolutionary leap that only 9 Ascended Masters had made up until August 2005. When fully transfigured, the master exits the human kingdom and enters the God-kingdom.

Testing: *Power*

We can surmise by looking at the third phases of the previous two stages that this stage's third phase also has something to do with power. The challenge here is to accumulate, harness and conserve enough power to shatter the glass-like shield that separates kingdoms. The master has to overcome the huge temptation of over-polarizing into the light: into the seasonless place of no emotion and great peace – the place of ultimate stagnation and inaction.

Changes:

The life-force center explodes during this phase, forming a large ball of life-force, slightly larger than the sphere of mental bodies. The spirit body's light fibers cluster into one rope extending from the assemblage point behind the shoulder blades, to the zero point portal that has formed behind the belly-button.

Challenge:

Ascended Masters have great perception. The greater our perception, the greater our emotions have to be. When emotions aren't recognized and utilized as the growth mechanisms they are, these very large emotions can be deliberately disconnected from in order to experience the peace of the bliss that plays through every cell at this point. But,

Hormonal Excretions that Hold the Higher Bliss

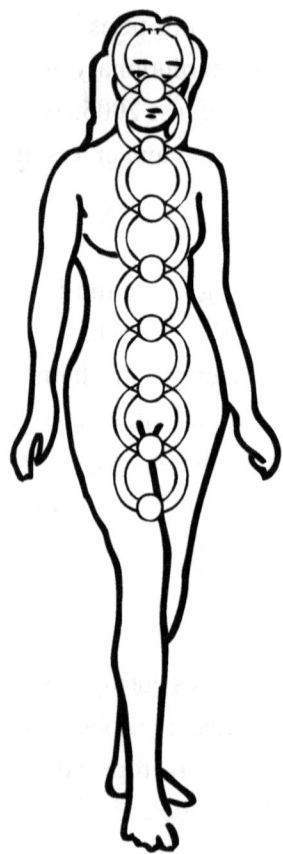

In the Immortal Master the alpha chakra (a hand length below the spine) and the second heart (on the sternum) are fully opened. The energy meridians move (sideways in women, front to back in men) through the centers where the chakras used to be before they formed a unified chakra field. The meridians end slightly above the pineal gland causing it to excrete life hormones for heightened bliss and immortality.

it is the power of emotion that will crack the 'glass' shield the master has to go through to get to the next kingdom. All chakras must be participating in creating this emotional response. Most Ascended Masters live only in the upper chakras. It becomes necessary to re-awaken the lower chakras, re-activate the sex drive and use it to arouse the other emotions. With the power of emotion, the shield shatters and the zero point opening explodes to fill all the fields. The fields around the body explode to double their size. The cord of light fibers now elongates and loops from the assemblage point on the outside edge of the fields to the heart center and back again to the assemblage point. The master has become a god-being in the flesh. (See illustration – *Within the God-kingdom.*)

Bodies of Man within the God-Kingdom

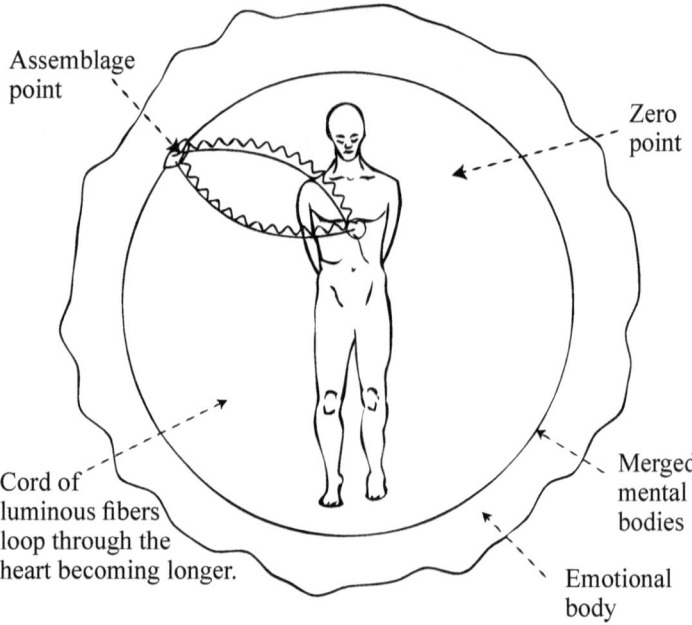

The God-kingdom: Future Destiny Of Man

A large leap of consciousness awaits man if he wishes to go beyond human boundaries. As we have seen, only 9 made it across this boundary before 2005.

Unlike the 3 stages within the human kingdom, the God-kingdom has two levels. It is essential that more and more humans enter the God-kingdom, as did Christ, Buddha, Krishna, Quan Yin and Sunat Kumara among others, because it is their destiny to change the inactivity found there. Humans are accustomed to struggle and a great struggle awaits in the God-kingdom to avoid succumbing to the inactivity and lack of growth in that realm. The struggle is against the huge enticement of bliss. Although we encounter bliss as a testing within the human stages, the bliss of this higher stage is eight times stronger. It becomes difficult to move even a limb and activity tends to slow almost to a standstill.

During the first phase of the God-kingdom, the fields around the body are very enlarged. The small zero point opening found behind the belly-button of an Ascended Master explodes as the transition to the God-kingdom is made. The zero point enlarges to fill the entire mental body, pushing the emotional body outside of the mental body.

The mental body (the sum total of all the mental bodies initially found in man, fused into one) starts to rotate. The cord of light fibers loops from the assemblage point through the heart and back again. During this phase emotions are felt much more intensely.

One of the main reasons the vast majority of Ascended Masters never enter here is because it requires pulsing the emotions between their positive and negative poles,[2] fueled by sexuality, to break the

---

[2] Following cosmic changes in December 2008, we no longer pulse between aspects as all fields, light, frequency, etc. are now blended. For more information see *Belvaspata, Angel Healing Volume I or II*.

glasslike membrane between the kingdoms – something shunned by Ascended Masters until recently.

The second phase of the God-kingdom is precipitated by yet another zero point explosion that pushes the mental body outside of the emotional body. The end result is a thin emotional body just inside the mental body, while the rest of the space is filled with the zero point. The clockwise and counter-clockwise movements of the mental body no longer make 360 degree rotations, but flip back and forth with just partial rotations. The cord of light fibers has to elongate to reach in a loop from the heart to the assemblage point on the enlarged mental body. Emotions dramatically diminish.

Gods have not reproduced themselves. Then on September 16, 2005, the god that is known as number 3 of the Alumuanu King's court, fathered twins. This was an event of such magnitude that it shot our cosmos up 38 levels, birthing twin rings of suns and planets around the outer rim of our cosmos. It also enabled gods to reproduce and catapulted our cosmos into the second phase of its equivalent of the God-kingdom.

Another cosmos in its God-kingdom entered us 12 days later, once again fathering rings of suns and representing the mating of gods. The suns had previously been governed by solar lords, but now the suns that were created were governed by gods birthed simultaneously within the suns.

To reach its God-hood, the cosmos, just like an Ascended Master, had to become very sexual. Sexual energy became heightened throughout the cosmos and reproduction increased. To prepare for its Supergod-hood however, sexuality transformed to being in love and once again it swept the cosmos.

For someone in God-hood, the ability to fall in love can provide the movement between the poles of the eight emotions, essential in getting the energy necessary for making the leap to Supergod-hood. In order to help the cosmos reach its state of being in love, the greatest love story of all time was revealed.

Part I The Philosophy of the Magic of the Nine Directions

43. Kihalshavur-misanach

The ninth direction follows the other eight directions of North, East, South and West, Above, Below, Without and Within. The ninth direction is the direction of Through. The eight directions represent form and space. The ninth direction represents formlessness and spacelessness. It creates the quality of transparency and leverages, through alchemy, reality from being painted on an opaque surface, to a reality of art on illuminated glass, making the colors come alive.

44. Ekra-selenutvavi

The matrix has been seen in the previous paradigm of existence, as a confinement and a restriction to self-expression. In this higher paradigm, it contains the ability to illuminate all spatial experience from within.

The 75 principles of Hadji-ka are the illuminating insights of the matrix that allow the inner light and frequency of form to shine through matter. The distinction between inner and outer becomes dissolved as the inner and outer move through one another, living the 9th direction.

The Wheel of the Ninth Direction
Fusion through Resonance

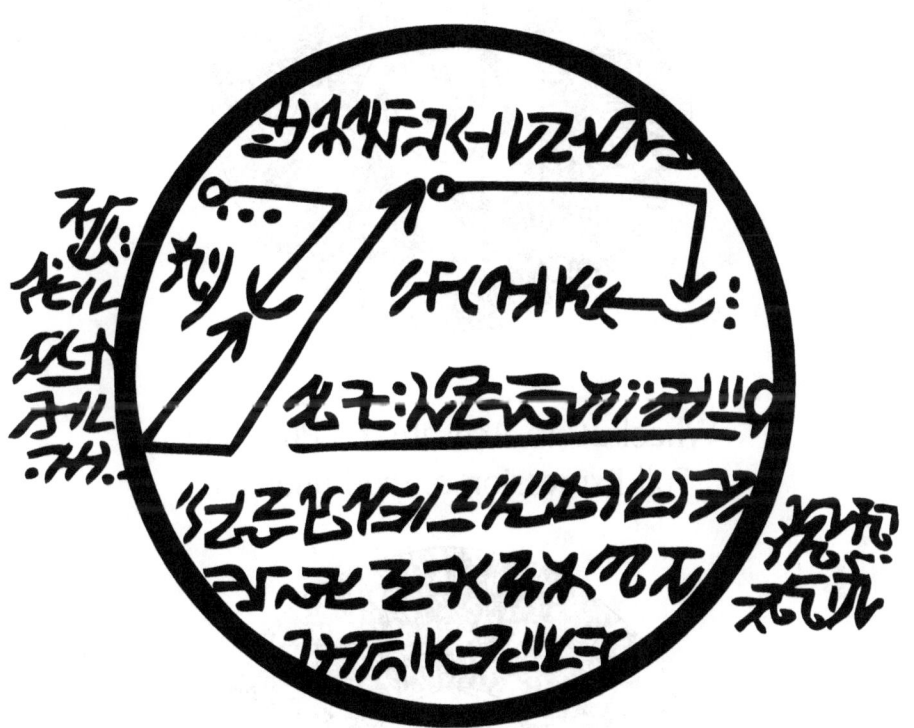

Nusba arut herchba nesevu

Wheel 19 to Activate the Pure and Full Expression of the Kundalini

Wheel 20 to Activate the Pure and Full Expression of the Kundalini

45. Kelesutvahut

The balancing of expression of the inner and outer, the feminine and masculine, is essential for this metamorphosis of existence to take place. The feminine has been less developed than the masculine and needs to have 3 illusions dissolved. In addition, it needs to have 3 insights acquired. The dissolving of illusions balances the masculine; the gaining of insights balances the feminine poles of the soul.

46. Virabitpahur-neska

The first illusion that has to be removed from the soul is that past injurious behavior from the masculine is something that will necessarily repeat itself. If past expectations dictate present defense mechanisms, we create a matrix that will confine us into cycles in which we encounter past events over and over again.

Wheel 21 to Activate the Pure and Full Expression of the Kundalini

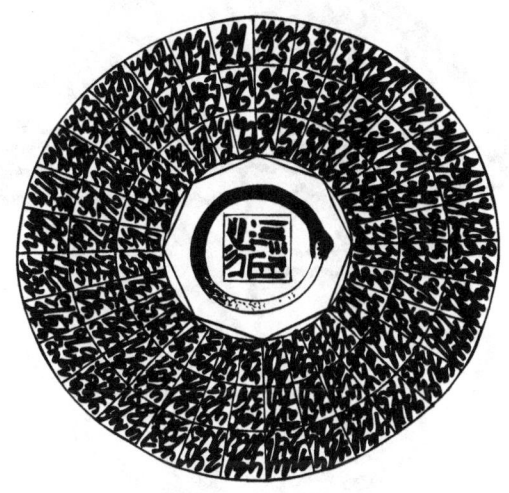

Wheel 22 to Activate the Pure and Full Expression of the Kundalini

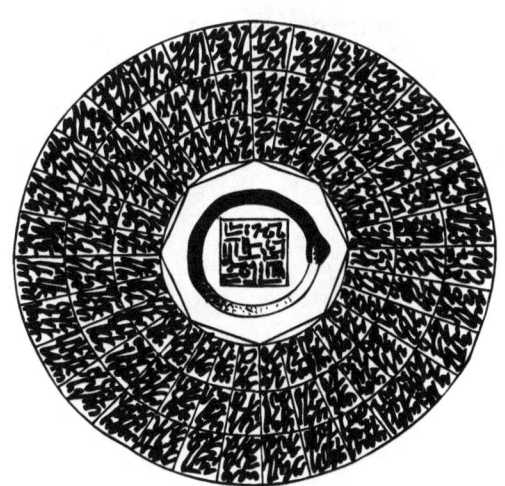

47. Retvi-ereklet-vanur

The second illusion to eliminate is the need for the feminine to prove that it can play the masculine role. Intuitive guidance competes with the masculine guidance of reason in steering life. Instinct too tries to tell us how to live. Reason deliberately contracts vision to get us to make mistakes so that we create karma to pull us back to physical life through rebirth. It is therefore not a reliable guidance source.

48. Plisarut-arsklahar

The heart's guidance is influenced by soul. It also uses our dreams to program our emotions in our daily life. Soul does not wish us success in our physical life. It wants us to voluntarily leave physicality in order to enter the soul reality. It provides flawed guidance through the heart, made worse by the neediness and insecurities we feel as we leave the dream state. The needs, wanting to be fulfilled, then masquerade as heart's guidance.

Wheel 23 to Activate the Pure and Full Expression of the Kundalini

Wheel 24 to Activate the Pure and Full Expression of the Kundalini

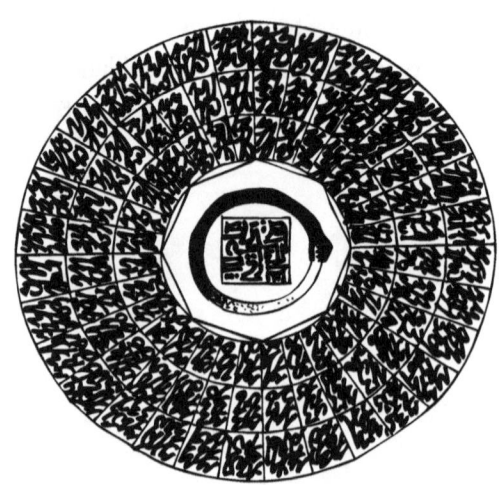

The Magical Practices of the Wheels of Hurat

The Symbol for the Wheels of Hurat

The 27 Wheels of Hurat

49. Krishkra-as-vartu

Instinctual guidance comes from spirit. Spirit tries to live physical life vicariously. Its role is as the canvas of existence, but instead it directs where the paint should go. It infiltrates not only the physical through mind control in the form of black light (subliminal information), but also interferes with the soul level of our dreams. It does not provide trustworthy guidance but dogma.

50. Misba-heres-tranavis

The third illusion that should be eliminated is the value placed on the ultra-feminine or the ultra-masculine, and the multi-layered programs associated with what the roles and identities of a man or a woman are. To over-polarize into any gender means that half of our expression needs to be suppressed. The ultra-masculine or ultra-feminine is therefore the most dysfunctional of all beings. The way we relate as a man or a woman is completely artificially programmed. The true nature of the interaction should be adventurous, child-like play and exploration of the subtle nuances of the alchemy of interaction.

51. *Plisba-kerekta-minavech*

The neutrality of allowing another's expression (alternating giving (+) and receiving (-) of expression) is the first insight of bringing balance to the feminine. Instead of thinking of itself as an independent unit that has to do everything itself, the feminine has to change its viewpoint to seeing itself as part of a family. It has to merge its existence with the positive and the neutral. The neutral can be thought of as its children (a boy and girl twins) and the positive as its husband, since it was the masculine and feminine separating that formed the neutral. The surrendering of the state of independence to the cohesive interaction of the family is like merging air, fire and sand to create transparent glass.

52. Virspa-esekla-verevit

The second insight for the feminine to achieve balance is that the true nature of living the ninth direction is for the masculine's expression to incorporate the feminine qualities and vice versa. The business meeting can be a wonderful candlelight dinner of beautifully prepared food eaten under the stars. In the silent moments of enjoyment, the compatibility of the partnership can be felt and unspoken agreements can be forged.

53. Sikva-miserech-uharestu

The combined interaction of the inner family with the masculine (physical) doing the eternal dance, the feminine (soul) playing the music and the neutral (spirit) providing the changing set, stage and props, creates the clarity for the Infinite's expression to be known. Without each trying to control the other's performance, opposition decreases and inevitable action reveals itself. The third insight of the feminine is that any guidance, other than the automatic and inevitable action that stems from being aligned with Infinite Intent, is unreliable.

54. Misech-blivabes-urespi

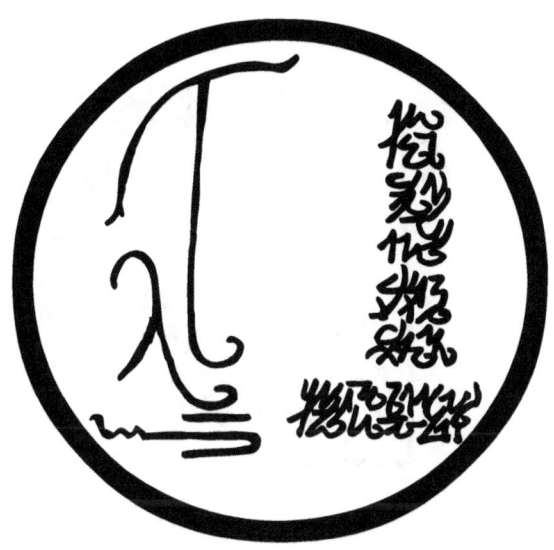

A great secret now we tell for those who want to understand how it is possible for life around them to be a mirror and how, to another, you are but a mirror: The secret to unlock this mystery is time. It rotates like a disc with each life form having a position on the disc. Wherever your awareness is focused on the disc is the present moment for you. Only those elements of existence you are focused on are real in that, only where your awareness is, can you access the patterns of possibilities of existence. Everything outside of your 'moment,' or your illuminated spot on the turning disc of time, is but an unreal shadow on the mirrored walls of your chrysalis.

55. Hirasta-bli-uvabet-unechvi

The fact that everyone's 'real' moment is on a different spot on the wheel of time means that we live in different realities and in different times. Each moment is real only because it is a spot that someone has become aware of by seeing the patterns of specific possibilities that stimulate action. This creates their reality. If we focus on another set of possibilities, we immediately change our reality.

56. Tri-urba-es-minavech

The reality we live in is therefore entirely our choice. It is the result of our eternal and indivisible self participating in the game of space and time. This is done by illuminating certain possibilities through focused awareness. Being 'stuck' in a certain situation in life is the result of a fixated mindset and perspective. Our attempting to know and understand, and the creating of belief systems to make it seem possible, fixate it.

57. Sekve-uselvavechspi

The cosmos itself is the Eternal Being's 'moment' – an eye of observation through which It observes Itself. But it is also just a spot on a bigger disc in a chain that never ends, for such is the nature of mirrors. There is only One Being that exists, that has contracted Its focused awareness into the Embodiment of the Infinite.

58. Trihur-manavesh-usekla

The cosmos, as a fixated perspective, has served the purpose of creating dense form – the more contracted a perspective is, the more it consists of dense forms. It has mapped the possibilities of a certain part of the Infinite Being. Man has the most contracted perspective, producing ego-identification, and of all species, is therefore the most dense.

59. Sihut-satamisut-akla

The denser a being is, the faster time flows and the shorter the life spans are. The way to expand time – the ability to accomplish many days' worth of work in one day – is to expand your awareness to a larger consciousness. See yourself as a being as vast as the cosmos having a human experience.

60. Virsevat-arahach-sufelvi

Both contraction and expansion provide equally valuable contributions. Man has a tendency to value the perception of less dense beings from 'higher' realms more than his own. Because they hold a bigger space through which life flows, they are able to see more at once. Man can only see what is in front of him and what is physical, but he can also see the depth of existence and has the highest developed analytical skills. He produces the questions; the higher realms can produce the answers by accessing the known.

61. Miskla-bravech-suhut-vabi

The newly accessed knowledge of the part of the Infinite's Being that is being examined by cosmic life comes through man. It is in his density where the unknowable filters into the known; where the depth of the flow of life is experienced. Like a wide river that is forced through a narrow chasm, not only does the narrow perspective and focus of man speed up time, but it also produces power beyond what can be experienced by the wide, slow river (the more etheric beings with a wide perspective).

62. Skahur-mesenechvi-aresta

It would seem that those who have gone into expanded awareness (like masters who have gone into god-consciousness) and beings in higher realms who live from a more expanded perspective, have a far more abundant life. There are many more opportunities and possibilities available to them because they are exposed to a lot more of the river of existence (the turning disc) through their larger space or moment. But with a wider perspective there is much overlooked, because the details are missed.

63. Nichsta-setlvu-heravi

The details of life are the indicators of when changes in direction are needed. They are doorways to open and explore, each leading into the deeper mysteries of existence. Key concepts of understanding are vested in the little details of existence because they are each a key to the unknowable contradiction of existence.

64. Kirsarach-spi-urpahet

Seers focus on the details when they find themselves facing overwhelming odds. This contracts their reality away from the chaotic circumstances surrounding them. If they contract it to a single point, they can cause time to stand still. Furthermore, this contraction creates more available power. They are also able to find the larger problem in the more manageable little details, since every cell contains the replica of the cosmos; the parts contain the whole.

65. Kretaa-mishuvit

The nine directions are nine perspectives within each being. This produces nine elements. The most contracted perspective produces matter. The change in elements is the result of a change in the frequency of the frequency component of the building blocks of existence. Perception (which is determined by perspective) yields frequency and vice versa. The density of form can be altered by perspective expanding or contracting.

66. Kersuch-niset-uvlehasbi

An example of times you may want to be fully physical is when you are wanting to enjoy physical sensuality, such as a warm bath, food, sexual stimulation, the grass beneath bare feet. When you are surrounded by dense circumstances, such as many constricting rules and regulations, and people with base motives, expansion allows it to move through you with only that which resonates sticking or lingering.

67. Elesmisarut-ukre

The fusion of all nine elements can only take place when all are equally valued. The physical has been more highly valued and has therefore kept us in bondage to mortality. It has created drama – pain, disease, hunger, cold and heat – to keep itself empowered by our focused attention. Its transformation, processes of eating and eliminating, awake times and regenerative sleep, provide a self-generated energy source. The other elements have fed off matter's energy, again focusing attention on it. Matter has kept its sovereignty by the attention focused on it.

Part I The Philosophy of the Magic of the Nine Directions

68. *Kirespartu-anunat*

The first four of the nine elements of existence are: The subatomic particles of matter, which resemble a wavy cross and the subatomic particles of energy, which resemble two interlocking spheres. These represent the south and the west respectively. The elements of life-force and power (representing the east and the north) are in the shape of little tube toruses that form inter-dimensional gateways between the two levels of spirit.

69. *Erchpa-uhusavespi*

The additional four elements are from different layers of akasha. These four elements form the horizontal, feminine axis of existence – that which holds memory. The previous four directions form the masculine, electrical and vertical axis that interprets memory through experience and perception. The four akashic records of memories, or layers, consist of firstly, the directions of above (where memories of 'what ifs' are kept) as the most etheric layer of akasha. The second most etheric layer of akasha is the direction of below (where the 'if onlys' are kept). The direction of within holds the records of emotions and the densest akashic layer, the direction of without, holds the record of actions.

70. Gli-urba-sehet-vanut

Memory determines shape. The feminine can manipulate reality by altering memory. The soul can therefore manipulate the body and physical life (the direction of the west can influence the direction of the south; energy can manipulate matter). The physical realms have therefore tried to reduce the soul's influence by becoming materialistic, by opposing it. In material life, opposites oppose. The result is more chaos.

71. Kererech-mishku-elsalvi

The pranic tube and the spine have separated, each acting independently. With energy and matter, opposites repel. The Ida and Pingala are etheric channels that twine like serpents through the center of the body – they are the tools of the two levels of spirit. They are +/– and –/+, but because they consist primarily of light and frequency, as opposites, they attract. In the layers of spirit, opposites inspire one another and therefore cooperate rather than repel, creating order rather than chaos.

Light and frequency (love) - opposites attract and sameness repels.

Energy and matter (physical) - sameness attracts and opposites repel.

The Ida and Pingala

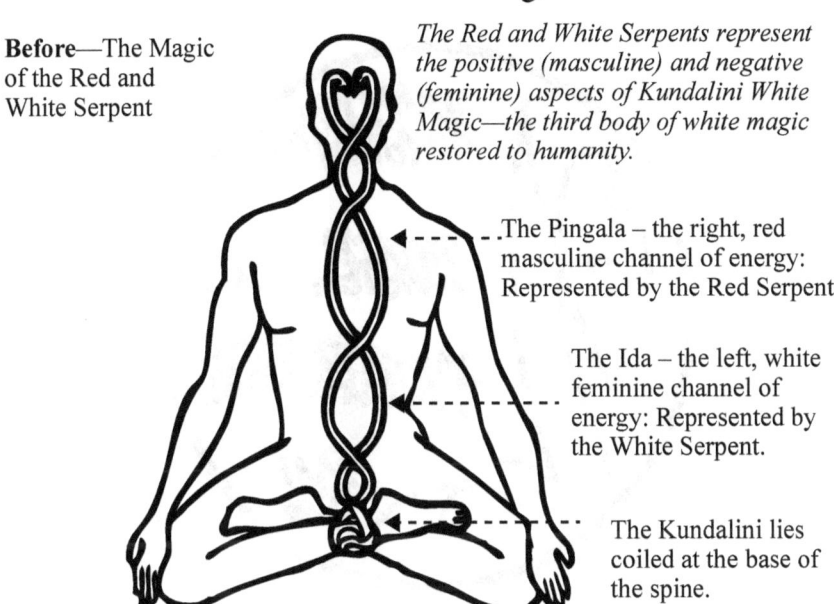

Before—The Magic of the Red and White Serpent

The Red and White Serpents represent the positive (masculine) and negative (feminine) aspects of Kundalini White Magic—the third body of white magic restored to humanity.

The Pingala – the right, red masculine channel of energy: Represented by the Red Serpent.

The Ida – the left, white feminine channel of energy: Represented by the White Serpent.

The Kundalini lies coiled at the base of the spine.

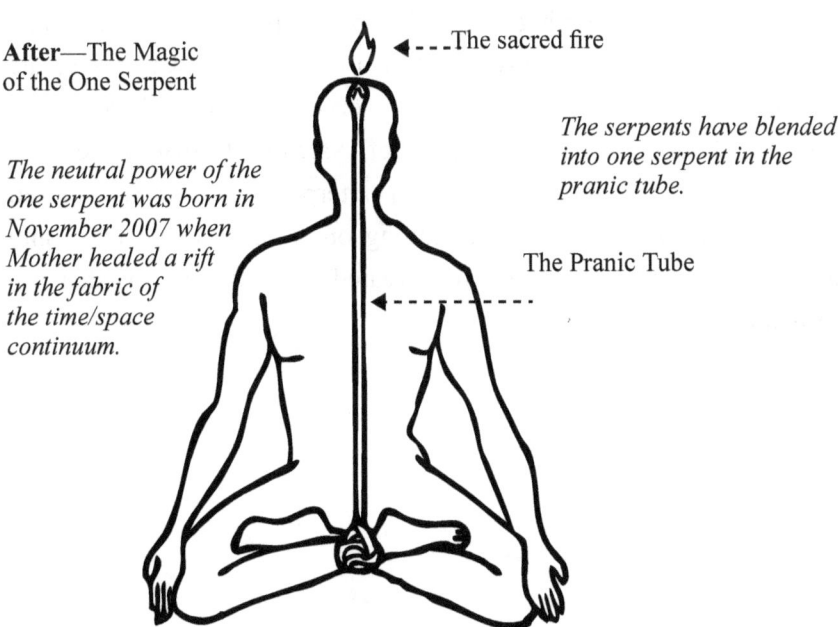

After—The Magic of the One Serpent

The neutral power of the one serpent was born in November 2007 when Mother healed a rift in the fabric of the time/space continuum.

The sacred fire

The serpents have blended into one serpent in the pranic tube.

The Pranic Tube

72. Tri-uranes-uklesut

The building blocks of the layers of spirit, the subatomic tube toruses, alternate in giving and taking between the two dimensional layers of spirit. The patterns of predictable outcome that they create are called order. Chaos and order each serve a purpose. Chaos breaks down old boundaries of existing belief systems. It creates questions that challenge the status quo. Order interprets the newly exposed information. Unfortunately our valuing order more than chaos, and answers more than questions, has created an overemphasis that has birthed the dogmatic tyranny of spirit.

73. Ska-ur-manaset-blivespi

The realms of spirit, as well as the two levels of the spirit of man, are made from akashic subatomic particles. The without and within are made of three interlocking wavy crosses and the above and below are made of three interlocking spheres. They have been governing the additional four directions' responses and realities through karmic memories held in their magnetic portions.

74. Sechvaa-vri-urbahur

The ninth direction of through is called the field of Infinite Intent. The subatomic particles of Infinite Intent resemble fluidly forming soap bubbles. They are larger than all the other particles that form the other directions. Their frequency component also vibrates at a higher speed. Frequency creates form and the higher frequencies override the form of the lower frequencies, thus, when fully lived and activated, it can exert greater influence on the formation of unfolding reality than that of the other directions that have kept life locked into a matrix of opposing factors.

75. Vesba-ur-neselvavi

The ninth direction's quality is *Fusion through Resonance*. Infinite Intent particles are called this because they can receive and interpret the changing changelessness of the Intent of the indivisible and eternal Source. They override the egoic will of all other building blocks by resonating with their eternal indivisible component and fusing with them. They override and encapsulate the smaller building blocks while infusing them with their true purpose: To be unique instruments of Infinite Expression.

"Life shall change and harmony shall come
When all life interprets the Intent of the One
Prepare now, let all that is stolen be restored
Be gone, all programs and memories from before

Prepare for the marriage of the direction of through
Release the dust of the ages that as personalities have accrued
The desire to control life must be released by you
To surrender to Source, this you must do

The hierarchies of old shall fall this day
The Infinite Intent shall lead the way
Renewed by the fusion, shall all life be
From the war of opposites you shall be free"

Part II

Practices of Dragon Magic

General Guidelines for Performing Ceremonies

The following are general guidelines for performing ceremonies. If specific directions are provided for any ceremony, use those directions; otherwise follow these general guidelines.

Creating and Dismantling a Ceremonial Circle

When creating a ceremonial circle, place the elements in a clockwise direction (on the floor or other surface). When dismantling the circle, pick up all the elements counter-clockwise.

Wheels, Squares, Triangles, Gates, etc as used in Ceremonies

When using elements such as Wheels, Triangles or Gates, the lowest numbers always go on top and the highest numbers on the bottom when these items are stacked. *Example:* Stack 1 is created at your head if you are lying down on your back or in front of your face if you are sitting. If each stack contains 8 Wheels then stack 1 contains Wheel 1–8 with lowest number on top and highest number on bottom; stack 2 contains Wheel 9–16, with lowest number on top and highest number on bottom — repeat this same order for each stack around the circle.

All ceremonial circles create an alchemical equation: Wheels or other items placed in stacks are created per the individual ceremony and create an alchemical equation that is different for each ceremony. Do not assume that you can determine the components of stacks for a ceremony with multiples of wheels, gates, etc.

The alchemy works through each item and thus it is important to stack them one upon another. This ensures that the components create the correct alchemical equation.

If the ceremony provides specific directions for creating stacks, follow them. All aspects of the alchemical equation have been considered by Almine as given in the specific instructions.

a. Item such as wheels, gates, squares, etc can be cut out singly. On some occasions when there are a large number of items, multiples may be placed on one page. As long as the elements are equally divided between the stacks and equally laid out on the pages — this is permissible. For example if there are 144 elements to be divided between 12 stacks, you may either have 2 elements per page or 4 elements per page. The types of elements should not be mixed when combining onto one page.
b. Ensure you follow the directions for creating the stacks needed for each of the ceremonies.
c. The shape of a circle must be maintained when creating the stacks.
d. If in doubt it is best to follow the exact ceremonial guidelines as given.
e. *With our intent to create the sacred space, we are part of the alchemical equation.* When following the ceremonial guidelines, we produce the known results of the alchemical equation that are intended for any specific ceremony.

Position

Lying down on your back is the preferred position. You may use a bed, a massage table or the floor. Ensure you are comfortable. It is okay to use a small pillow under your knees and your head or neck.

Follow the directions as given for each specific ceremony. For the majority of these ceremonies, your head should be placed at the Number 1 Wheel or Stack (which correlates to 12 on the clock). If you choose to sit on a chair, the Number 1 Wheel or Stack should be placed in front of you.

Creating Sacred Space

Avoid interruptions of any sort as you create your sacred space and participate in your ceremony, whether it is a physical ceremony or one of intent. Once you start the ceremony it is best to complete it. (Unplug the phone, go to the restroom, etc - prior to starting.)

Ceremonies build upon each other. It is recommended that they be completed in the order given. Ceremonies may be repeated as often as you feel is appropriate and right for you.

Note: Maintain the sacred space and circle — keep animals and children out of the area by closing doors, etc. The frequency of the sacred circle is affected by their presence and they are affected by the ceremonial frequencies. These frequencies may be too high for them.

Recommendations during pregnancy: The frequencies of a ceremony may be too high for the baby and therefore, not comfortable. As a general rule, avoid doing ceremonies during pregnancy.

The Use of Wheels

A wheel is a visual image that conveys non-cognitive, sacred and empowering information. They are similar to gateways through which specific healing frequencies are drawn and are power sources in the same way a holy object would be.

The wheels are alive and as we work with them they provide us with deep insights into the vastness and wealth of our own being, reminding us of all that we are.

Each wheel is a stand-alone wheel and can be used by itself. When wheels are used in a sequence, they tell a story and combine to make an equation.

Mystical practices have a beginning and a closure. If you are working with a sequence of wheels, do not stop in the middle as it leaks resources and energy. For this reason it is important that you always complete each sequence.

To access the information contained within the wheels at a deeper level you may place your hands on the wheels or run your hand across them — the left hand is receptive and the right hand promotes understanding.

Lying down, you may also place a wheel at your feet and upon contemplating its meaning, bring it up through your body from your feet to the Lahun Chakra 10 inches above your head. If a wheel feels 'stuck' anywhere, continue to feel the quality of the wheel until it moves freely. If you are working with a sequence of wheels, ensure that the highest numbered wheel is at the bottom and the lowest numbered wheel is at the top. Work with one wheel at a time and fully integrate one before moving on to the next. As you do, also contemplate how the qualities of each wheel combine and complement the other wheels within the sequence.

Possible Uses for Wheels include:
- Meditate on a wheel.
- Place on the walls of a healing space, office or a room in which you spend a lot of time.
- With intention they can be placed into the body or placed directly on the body.
- Specific wheels can be placed under a healing table when working on someone or under a chair that you frequently sit on.
- Create your own personal mandala that you carry with you.

The Ceremony to Clear Programs from the Spine

Pre-meditation

- Place yourself in a deeply meditative state.
- From a large perspective, view your interactions with others and the personality traits you use to shield yourself, control outcomes or to make yourself needed, wanted or accepted. See these personality traits as masks – learned behaviors that have accumulated over lifetimes.
- See these masks disintegrate like dust and blow away in the wind. Continue until only authenticity remains.
- Now do the same clearing process with the inner personalities – the personas; the way you interact with yourself. The masks you wear for yourself. See them melt and flow away like water as you identify and dissolve them one by one.
- As you end the meditation, envision how your life will be lived without the masks of personality. You are now ready for the ceremony.

Creating the Ceremonial Space

Using the following items, create a ceremonial stack to place at your feet:

Place *The Wheel of the Ninth Direction* at the bottom of the stack.

Then the *The Nervous System Maps* in the following order:

1) *The Nervous System Map to Seal the Interdimensional Holes of the Sacrum*
2) *The Nervous System Map to Seal the Interdimensional Holes of the Coccyx*
3) *The Nervous System Map to Seal the Interdimensional Holes of the Brain Stem*

On top of that place the *24 Maps to Clear the Nervous System,* starting with Map 24 at the bottom and ending with Map 1 on top.

You may want to have a list of the elements that make up the stack so you can contemplate their purpose as you draw them up through your body.

The Ceremony

- As you begin the ceremony, again contemplate existing without masks, personalities, and coping mechanism. Focus being as open and trusting as a child.
- Envision the power images moving up through your body one by one, starting with the first and uppermost image – Map 1 for Clearing of the Nervous System. Move each one in turn, in through the bottom of the feet, up through your body and out through the top of your head. When one image has fully moved through, envision the next one moving through. Pay particular attention to

the feeling of clearing the 'cobwebs' of programming from the spine.
- If you feel pressure building in a specific area as though a power image has become stuck, breath deeply in and out and release the programs from that area on the out-breath. Silently say, "I release" several times until the power image moves through and out.

When you have completed the ceremony, close it by acknowledging your gratitude and pick up all power images. Recognize the sacredness of the ceremony and the tools.

The Ceremony to Clear the Programs from the Pranic Tube

Pre-meditation

Note: *In clearing the inner and outer personalities, specifically focus on personalities and identities that are connected to emotions (i.e. I am the friendly one, the optimistic one, etc.)*

- Place yourself in a deeply meditative state.
- From a large perspective, view your interactions with others and the personality traits you use to shield yourself, control outcomes or make yourself needed, wanted or accepted. See these personality traits as masks – learned behaviors that have accumulated over lifetimes.
- See these masks disintegrate like dust and blow away in the wind. Continue until only authenticity remains.
- Now do the same clearing process with the inner personalities – the personas; the way you interact with yourself. The masks you wear for yourself. See them melt and flow away like water as you identify and dissolve them one by one.
- As you end the meditation, envision how your life will be lived without the masks of personality. You are now ready for the ceremony.

Creating the Ceremonial Space

Using the following items, create a ceremonial stack to place at your feet:

Place *The Wheel of the Ninth Direction* at the bottom of the stack.

Then place *The Power Sigil to restore all Parts of the Body, Soul, Spirit and Akasha to their Proper Places.*

At the top of the stack place *The 24 Wheels to Activate the Pure and Full Expression of the Kundalini* (Wheel 24 is at the bottom and Wheel 1 is at the top).

You may want to have a list of the elements that make up the stack so you can contemplate their purpose as you draw them up through your body.

The Ceremony
- Lie comfortably with the stack of power images at your feet.
- As you begin the ceremony, again contemplate existing without masks, personalities, and coping mechanism. Focus on being as open and trusting as a child.
- Envision the power images moving up through your body one by one, starting with the first and uppermost image – Wheel 1 to Activate the Pure and Full Expression of the Kundalini. Move each one in turn, in through the bottom of the feet, up through your body and out through the top of your head. When one image has fully moved through, envision the next one moving through in the same way. Pay particular attention to the feeling of clearing the 'cobwebs' of programming from the spine.

- If you feel pressure building in a specific area as though a power image has become stuck, breath deeply in and out and release the programs from that area on the out-breath. Silently say, "I release," several times until the power image moves through and out.

When you have completed the ceremony, close it by acknowledging your gratitude and pick up all power images. Recognize the sacredness of the ceremony and the tools.

The Power Sigil to Restore all Parts of the Body, Soul, Spirit and Akasha to their Proper Places

The Ceremony to Clear the Ida and Pingala – the Instruments of Spirit

Pre-meditation:
- Place yourself in a meditative state and scan the areas of your life where you have made people, institutions or principles 'holy'.
- Release all by visualizing them dissolving into the eternal ocean. Release any judgments you may have of worthiness. One part of the river is not worth more than another – they both ultimately dissolve into the mighty ocean.
- Make the statement, "I release all programs from spirit about what is holy or unholy".

Creating the Ceremonial Space

Using the following items, create a ceremonial stack to place at your feet:

Place *The Wheel of the Ninth Direction* at the bottom of the stack.

Then place *The Power Wheel of Spirit.*

On top of the stack place *The Sigils for Balancing Spirit.*

Using the *27 Wheels of Hurat,* create a clockwise circle, big enough for you to line in. Wheel 1 will be above your head as you lie down.

You will need a list of the 27 Angels of Spirit and their Sigils to call upon during the ceremony. You may want to have a list of the elements that make up the stack so you can contemplate their purpose as you draw them up through your body.

The Ceremony
- When you are ready, lie down in the ceremonial space, ensuring that you are comfortable. Remember Wheel 1 is above your head.
- Call out the 27 Angel names as you look at their sigils and instruct them to remove all spirit infiltration and programs from your body and soul.
- Next instruct them to remove all physical and soul infiltration and control of spirit.
- Then, starting with the image on the top of the stack at your feet – ***The Sigils for Balancing Spirit,*** envision moving all the sacred images up through your body, one at a time, and out of the top of your head.

- If you feel pressure building in a specific area as thought a power image has become stuck, breath deeply in and out and release the programs from that area on the out breathe.
- End with these words: "Let all aspects of expression of my being be aligned with Infinite Intent."

When you have completed the ceremony, close it by acknowledging your gratitude and pick up all power images. The Wheels of Hurat are dismantled in a counter-clockwise direction. Recognize the sacredness of the ceremony and the tools.

The Power Wheel of Spirit

The Sigils for Balancing Spirit
Order within Fluidity

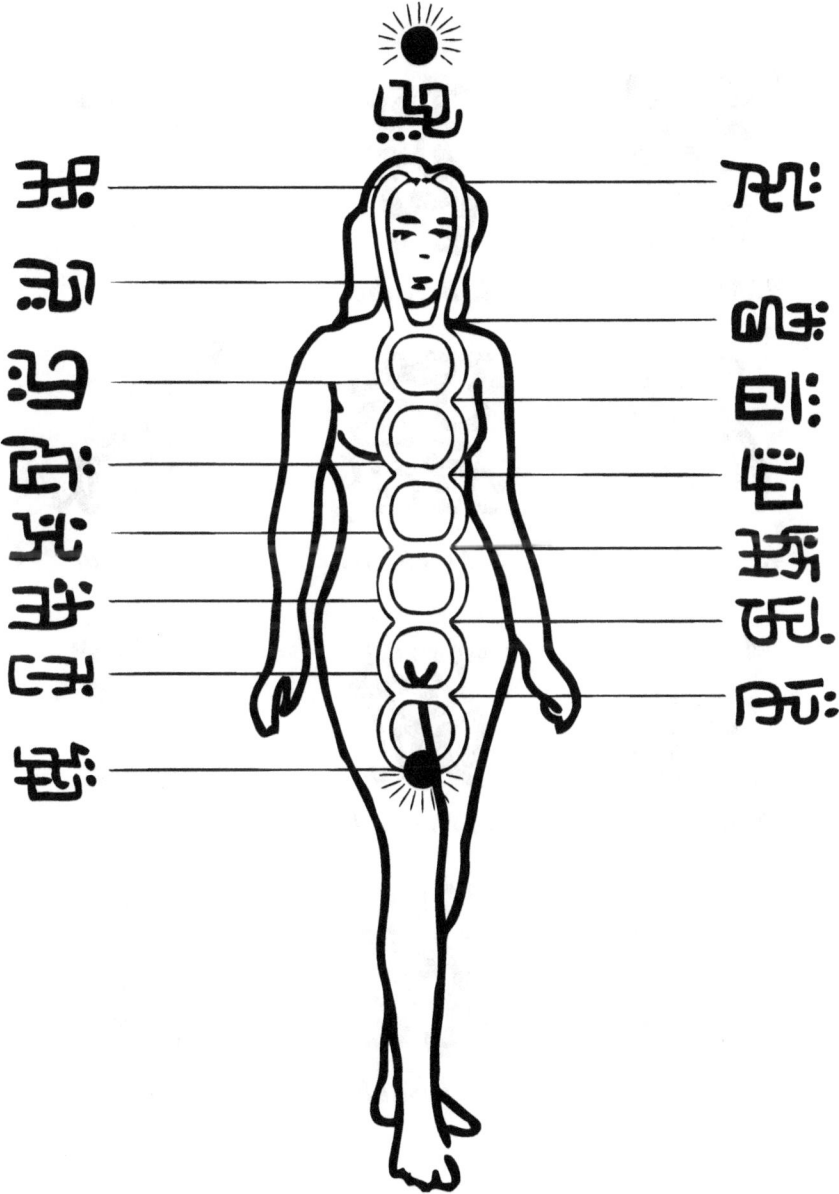

The 27 Angels of Spirit and their Sigils

1. Mananut

2. Brivahet

3. Silvatu

4. Kershvavi

5. Mechbaru

6. Kirasat

7. Kletvatu

8. Nevarek

9. Kusavi

10. Kletvaru

11. Bishalvi

12. Mesuk

Part II Practices of Dragon Magic

13. *Nektuva*

14. *Reksalvavi*

15. *Nanaruk*

16. *Echtuvar*

17. *Litselvi*

18. *Ramavek*

19. *Harsvarut*

20. *Kliharasat*

21. *Nenesut*

22. *Marstuve*

23. *Neksuvalvi*

24. *Rakbahur*

25. *Nanusak*

26. *Rasbarut*

27. *Melsakvi*

The Ceremony to Restore the Missing Codes of the Four Directions

The Blending of Directions 1, 2, 3, 4 with 5, 6, 7, 8

(See the Diagram of the Qualities of the Eight Directions)

Pre-meditation:

Contemplate the following: The akashic records are the 'storage' places (realities) of lost codes from the four directions. There are only four directions, with lost pieces making up the additional four directions. The codes that have been lost, or left behind, are the building blocks called 'akasha'. They are either three interlocking spheres or three interlocking wavy lines.

When these lost pieces are restored to the four directions, they become a fusion of building blocks: Incorruptible Matter.

The Qualities of the Eight Directions

Directions 1 – 4	Directions 5 – 8
Building Blocks: Light, Frequency, Energy, Power	**Building Blocks:** 4 layers of Akashic Records
↓ **1. Masculine layer of Spirit** North *Quality*: Uniformity – dependence, tribalism	↑ **8. Akashic Records of Hopes ('What ifs')** Above *Quality*: Absolute Oneness – full empathic and telepathic connection
↓ **2. Feminine Layer of Spirit** East *Quality*: Co-dependence	↑ **7. Akashic Records of Regrets ('If onlys')** – Below *Quality*: Supported Diversity
↓ **3. Soul** West *Quality*: Independence	↑ **6. Akashic Records of Emotions** Within *Quality*: Self-sovereignty
↓ **4. Physicality** South *Quality*: Unity within Diversity – one-mindedness	↑ **5. Akashic Records of Deeds** Without *Quality*: Diversity within unity – one heartedness

Creating the Ceremonial Space

Firstly the codes, or building blocks, must be cleansed before restoration. They have held old memories of various degrees of distortion.

During the ceremony you will be lying comfortably with the following stack of power images at your feet.

To create the stack:

Place *The Power Wheel for the Joining of the Akaskic Layers with the Four Directions* at the bottom of the stack.

Then place *The 8 Alchemical Equations* (Equation 8 is at the bottom and Equation 1 is at the top).

On top of the Equations place *The Wheel to Cleanse the Akaska.*

You will need a list of the *Names and Sigils of the Angels of the Eight Directions* to call upon during the ceremony. You may also want to have a list of the elements that make up the stack so you may contemplate their purpose as you draw them up through your body.

The Ceremony

- Lie comfortably on your back with the stack of sacred images at your feet. Call upon the angels of the eight directions as you look at their sigils. Instruct them to move the sacred wheels and equations through your body one by one, starting with the image at the top – ***The Wheel to Cleanse the Akasha.***
- One by one, envision the top wheel, the eight equations and then the power wheel, move up through your body and out the top of your head.

- If you feel pressure building in a specific area, as though a power image has become stuck, breath deeply in and out and release the programs from that area on the out-breath.
- Feel the silence in your body as you end the ceremony by saying:

    Reveshut aharch pravasbi
    My being dwells in timelessness

When you have completed the ceremony, close it by acknowledging your gratitude and pick up all power images. Recognize the sacredness of the ceremony and the tools.

Part II Practices of Dragon Magic

The Angels of the Eight Directions

1. Netararek

2. Bluvatrasut

3. Menachve

4. Kalsbararuk

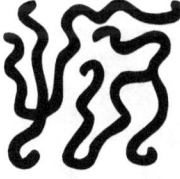

5. Mihavaruk

6. Nesevasvi

7. Priha-uvasut

8. Nesabavet

The Power Wheel for the Joining of the Akashic Layers with the Four Directions

Chevavich Unasve Minusit

Part II Practices of Dragon Magic

The Wheel to Cleanse the Akasha

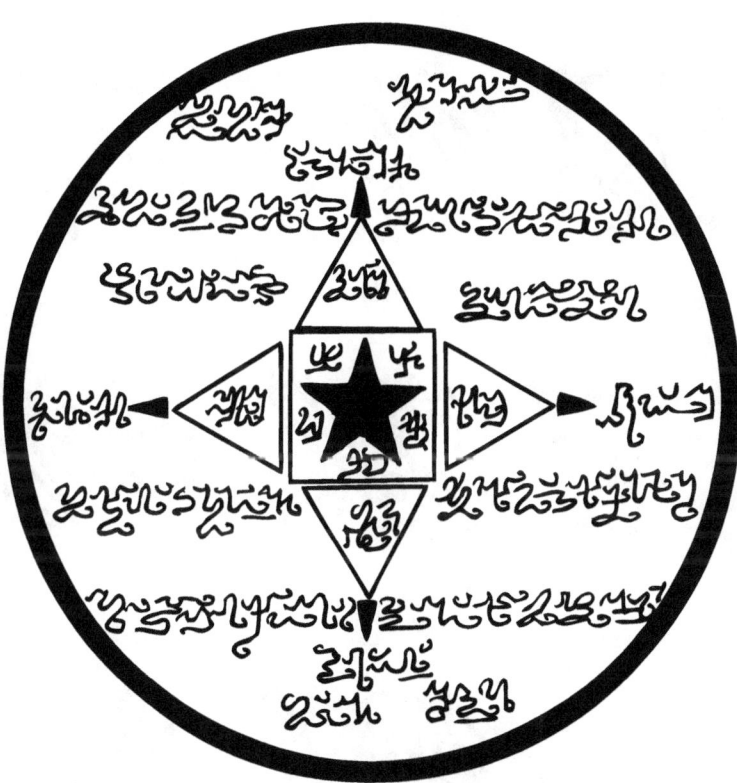

The Emotional Reparation of the Four Directions
Alchemical Equation I

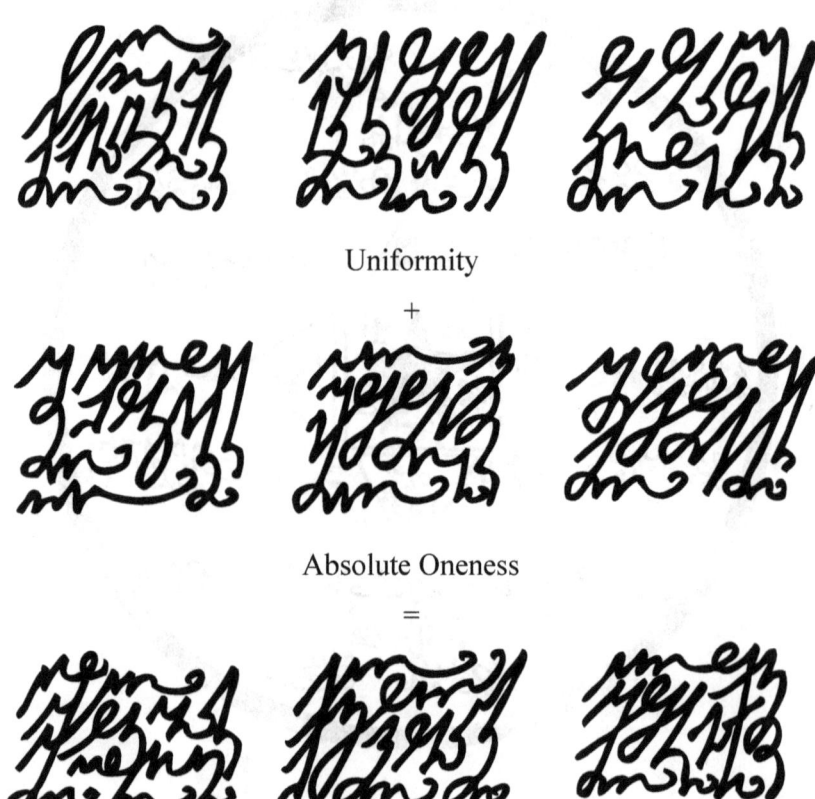

Uniformity

+

Absolute Oneness

=

Empathic and Telepathic Inclusiveness

The Emotional Reparation of the Four Directions
Alchemical Equation 2

Co-dependence

+

Supported Diversity

=

Mutual Inspiration

The Emotional Reparation of the Four Directions
Alchemical Equation 3

Independence

+

Self-sovereignty

=

Independent Self-sovereignty

Part II Practices of Dragon Magic

The Emotional Reparation of the Four Directions
Alchemical Equation 4

Unity within Diversity

+

Diversity within Unity

=

Unity within Harmony

The Alchemical Equations of the Resurrection
Alchemical Equation 5

Unity within Harmony

+

Independent Self-sovereignty

=

The Joyful Adventure of the One Expressing as the Many

The Alchemical Equations of the Resurrection
Alchemical Equation 6

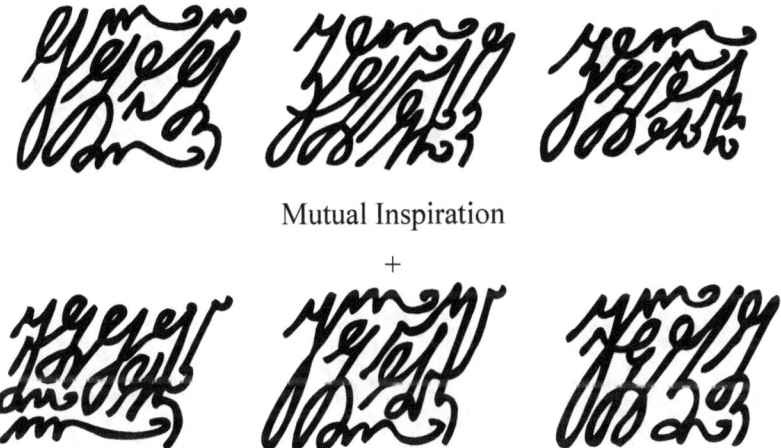

Mutual Inspiration

+

Empathic and Telepathic Inclusiveness

=

The Harmonious Interaction of the Many Expressing as One

The Alchemical Equations of the Resurrection
Alchemical Equation 7

The Joyful Adventure of the One Expressing as the Many

+

The Harmonious Interaction of the Many Expressing as One

=

The Contented Peace of Reclaimed Wholeness

Part II Practices of Dragon Magic

The Alchemical Equations of the Resurrection
Alchemical Equation 8

The Contented Peace of Reclaimed Wholeness

+

Complete Alignment with Divine Intent

=

Fusion through Resonance into a Perfected Instrument of Divine Expression

The Ceremony for the Fusion of the Four Directions

Pre-meditation:

- Place yourself in a meditative state.
- Meditate on the harmlessness of all aspects of existence; how even infiltration of one aspect by another is but the result of our valuing one part of the opposites more than another. Contemplate how every aspect of existence is simply playing its part and only becomes a tyrant or a dictator when we judge any part of life as having more value than another.
- Scan your life and see all the places where you value and see as more real, one opposite over another. Allow value judgments of good and bad to disintegrate, like clay turning into dust and blowing away in the wind. Feel yourself to be as clear as a child who sees the beauty of the serpent the same as he does the beauty of the rose.
- Go into deep relaxation, by going backwards into the crystal clear waters of the blissful peace of your being.

Creating the Ceremonial Space

Around the space where you will be lying, create three circles of images and a stack of images that will lie at your feet. Ensure that the circle is large enough for you to lie in.

Inner Circle

Create the inner circle with the *24 Wheels of Veshba.* They will be in stacks of 2. Place wheel 1 and 2 above your head and lay out the 12 pairs of wheels around you in a clockwise circle. (The **lowest** numbered wheel in each stack is always on top.)

Middle Circle

Create the middle circle with the *24 Wheels of Manasuch.* It also consists of 12 stacks with 2 wheels in each. The stack with Wheels 1 & 2 will be above your head.

Outer Circle

Create the outer circle with the *27 Wheels of Hurat.* Lay them around the outside of the other two circles in a clockwise manner. These wheels are laid out singly to create a larger circle.

Stack at Feet

Now create the stack that goes at the bottom of your feet by placing the images in the following order and placing them one on top of the next:

The Fused Transparency of Body, Soul and Spirit

The Power Wheel of Spirit

The Power Sigil to Restore all parts of Body, Soul, Spirit and Akasha to their Proper Places

The Sigils for Balancing Spirit

The 27 Angels of Spirit and their Sigils

The Wheel of the Balanced Self-Sovereignty of Soul

The Map of the Nervous System to Seal the Interdimensional Holes of the Sacrum

The Map of the Nervous System to Seal the Interdimensional Holes of the Coccyx

The Map of the Nervous System to Seal the Interdimensional Holes of the Brain Stem

The Wheel – *The Fused Transparency of Body, Soul and Spirit* will be at the bottom and *The Map of the Nervous System to Seal the Interdimensional Holes of the Brain Stem* will be at the top.

Have a list beside you of the names and sigils for the *Pranic Tube Sigils of Merging* and the sigil for *Menekvi - Angel of Oneness of Spirit*.

The Ceremony

While in deep meditation, envision the holy marriage and romance of your masculine and feminine taking place through mutual surrender:

1. Speak the words:

   Irakva menuvish arasva minasut
   Complete transparency through fusion

2. Look at the sigils of the *Pranic Tube Merging* as you call their names. See the combined pranic tube and spinal cord glowing together inside the spine.

3. Next see the coiling serpents of the Ida and Pingala twining around the combined spine and pranic tube. See them start to

merge together as the masculine Pingala merges with the feminine Ida.

Say these words:

Machtu Anachve Hurasbi Sperare
Dynamic balance through Oneness

4. Call upon the ***Angel of Oneness of Spirit: Menekvi,*** while looking at his sigil, and instruct him to merge the Ida and Pingala.

5. Next, see the glowing, joined Ida and Pingala fuse with the joined pranic tube and spinal cord. All four will now fuse inside the spine, glowing as one inside and around the spine.

6. End this ceremony with the declaration:

Let the fusion of body, soul and both aspects of spirit, create the tool of resurrected, eternal matter. May this refined instrument of my being, dance to the symphony of Infinite Intent.

Erekvi Subavat Ereshvi
According to Divine Will

When you have completed the ceremony, close it by acknowledging your gratitude and pick up all power images. Recognize the sacredness of the ceremony and the tools. The images that make up the circles are dismantled in a counter-clockwise direction.

The Wheel of the Balanced Self-Sovereignty of Soul

The Fused Transparency of Body, Soul and Spirit

The Sigil of the Angel Menekvi

Kavala Sparut Helsachvi

Part II Practices of Dragon Magic

The Names of the Sigils for the Merging of the Pranic Tube

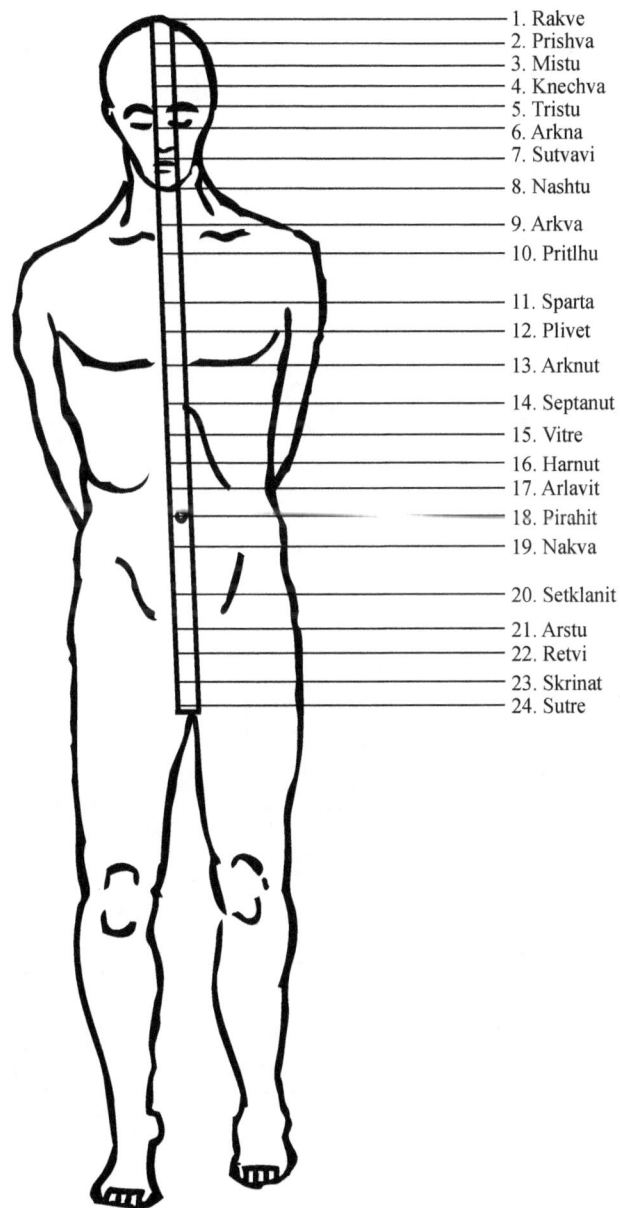

1. Rakve
2. Prishva
3. Mistu
4. Knechva
5. Tristu
6. Arkna
7. Sutvavi
8. Nashtu
9. Arkva
10. Pritlhu
11. Sparta
12. Plivet
13. Arknut
14. Septanut
15. Vitre
16. Harnut
17. Arlavit
18. Pirahit
19. Nakva
20. Setklanit
21. Arstu
22. Retvi
23. Skrinat
24. Sutre

The Seven Breaths of Eternal Life

The Pranic Tube Sigils of Merging

1. *Rakve* 2. *Prishva* 3. *Mistu*

4. *Knechva* 5. *Tristu* 6. *Arkna*

7. *Sutvavi* 8. *Nashtu* 9. *Arkva*

10. *Pritlhu* 11. *Sparta* 12. *Plivet*

Part II Practices of Dragon Magic

13. *Arknut*   14. *Septanut*   15. *Vitre*

16. *Harnut*   17. *Arlavit*   18. *Pirahit*

19. *Nakva*   20. *Setklanit*   21. *Arstu*

22. *Retvi*   23. *Skrinat*   24. *Sutre*

The Ceremony to Fuse the Combined Eight Directions with the Ninth Direction

Pre-meditation:

Place yourself in a deep meditative state. Ponder the following statements by feeling their meaning with your whole being:

1. I am a current in the Infinite ocean. It flows through me and I flow through it.

2. No external soul or spirit pieces of me exist. They are but unresolved imaginings of separation. I am eternal, inseparable and whole.

Creating the Ceremonial Space

During the ceremony you will be lying comfortably with the following stack of power images at your feet.

To create the stack:

Place *The Wheel of the Ninth Direction* at the bottom of the stack.

Then place *The 8 Alchemical Equations* (Equation 8 is at the bottom and Equation 1 is at the top).

On top of the Equations, place *The Power Sigil to Restore all parts of Body, Soul, Spirit and Akasha to their Proper Places*.

Finally, place *The Symbol for the Wheels of Hurat*, then *The Symbol for the Wheels of Manasuch* and lastly *The Symbol for the Wheels of Veshba*.

You will need a list of the *Names and Sigils for the Completion of the Cosmic Loops of Time* to call upon during the ceremony.

The Ceremony

1. As you are lying comfortably with the stack of power images at your feet, call upon by name, the 4 angels for the **Completion of the Cosmic Loops of Time** (while looking at their sigils).

2. Instruct them to move the symbols, equations and wheels that are in the stack, through your body – starting with the image at the top – **The Symbol for the Wheel of Veshba** – and then one at a time until you get to the last image.

3. If you feel pressure building in a specific area as though a power image has become stuck, breathe in and out deeply and release the programs from that area on the out-breath.

4. End by saying:

    Sabahut urachvi mishet vivavi

    The dream of separation is over

    May my being express fully, and without the unwholeness of gender, the Infinite splendor of eternal existence.

When you have completed ceremony, close it by acknowledging your gratitude and pick up all power images. Recognize the sacredness of the ceremony and the tools.

Part II Practices of Dragon Magic

Angels for the Completion of Cosmic Loop of Time

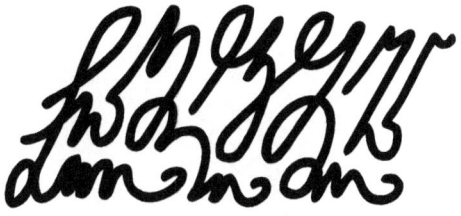

1. Meshperek-ratvi

2. Uhurusat-miravek

3. Blishpekvi-mirarak

4. Trekvarhus-aseta

The Four Loops of Existence Within the Fall

(Excerpt from Windows Into Eternity)

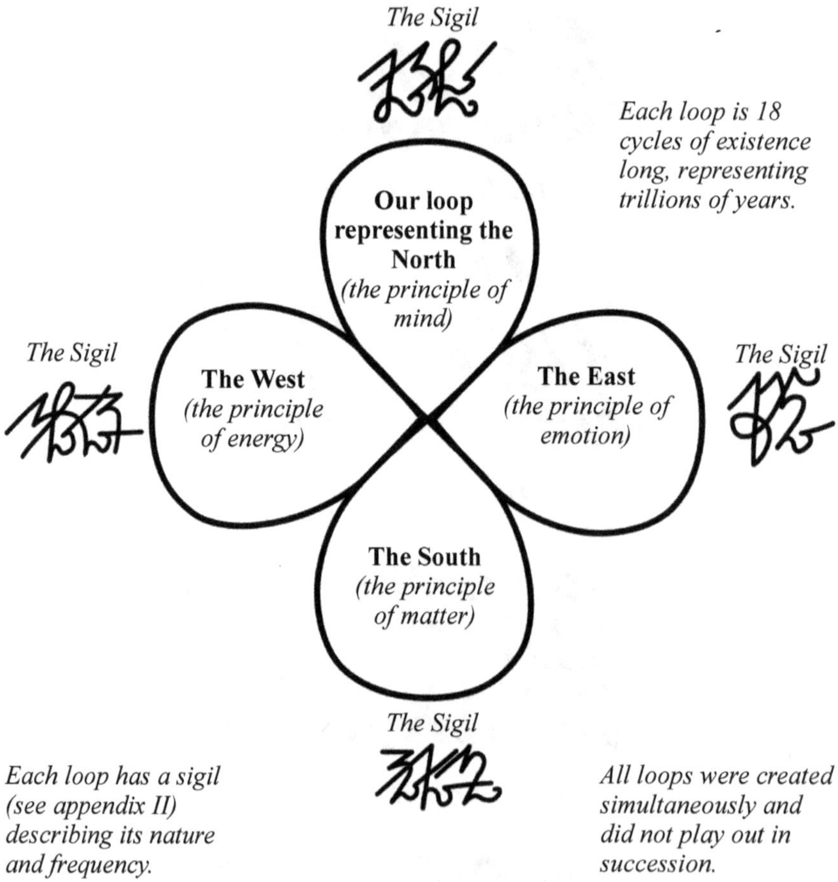

The Sigil

Our loop representing the North
(the principle of mind)

Each loop is 18 cycles of existence long, representing trillions of years.

The Sigil

The West
(the principle of energy)

The East
(the principle of emotion)

The Sigil

The South
(the principle of matter)

The Sigil

Each loop has a sigil (see appendix II) describing its nature and frequency.

All loops were created simultaneously and did not play out in succession.

The name for All Four Loops is: Kelesh-usva-trabach-heruhit

In Janauary, 2007, after successfully completing its ascension cycles, our loop in the north had all other loops join with it into one.

Closing

We stand at the closing of the four great loops of time. Over and over have we traveled them in search of long-lost pieces of expression. In finding them, we find our wholeness and reclaim the powerful, magical components that are our birthright.

The kingdom of the dragons has always waited at the closure of the specific loop we have now, yet again, completed. It is here that they have released the ancient records of the way to reclaim our magical abilities. It has been done according to the exact measure we are prepared to receive.

May our hearts embrace this most precious gift and the body respond to these long-kept secrets of how to release the powers of Hadji-ka – the sacred fire within us, that we can awaken the pristine, incorruptible magic of life.

Gender can only exist in the absence of expression of some of our aspects. In wholeness, the concept of gender becomes meaningless.

~ Almine

Part III

The 144 Precepts of the Higher Life

Precepts of the
Path to Freedom

1. I Am Home

Rachba-turarak-anish

Angel name: *Blisinatvi-pruvatu*

The only truth you can ever create is to expose through recognition, the pristine expression of the Infinite.

2. I Wait in Stillness

Bliva-hurasat-manit

Angel name: *Kurivanat-ersat*

The fairness of existence is unquestionable. Unfairness only arises from our inability to receive.

3. Opportunity is at the Door

Blespa-uhur-askretvi

Angel name: *Helevisinat-mechtunat*

Blessings can only come where density previously existed. Resisting density keeps it in place, preventing blessings from flowing into your life.

4. Knowing Right Action

Machba-prereret-uhusba

Angel name: *Karasetvi-halsatur*

Obsessions with raising the consciousness of the body, creates over-polarization into gravity. Living from the eternal self, expresses both the roots of gravity and the wings of levitation.

5. Look Behind Appearances

Berebishpa-mesenech

Angel name: *Mininatvi-sivar*

When we overvalue the etheric realms we have an existence of levitation, neglecting gravitation. This self-abandonment causes addictions.

6. Transition to Peace

Rekpa-blispater-anachvi

Angel name: *Kurat-pritinut*

Guilt comes through belief systems. Right action is always inevitable, whether we can see its value or not. All life therefore unfolds in innocence.

7. Spontaneous Expression

Restu-aklat-brihespa

Angel name: *Li-esetar-bravi*

In the child, the adult slumbers. In the mortality of humans, godhood sleeps, to awaken like the seed with the song of spring.

8. Endless Possibilities

Ninavech-setvi-beshpava

Angel name: *Kasahetvi-blavi*

Self-reflection contains the element of comparison, which provides opposition by creating in others a mirror. Self-examination uses multi-perspectives to ensure that clarity and truth are the origins of our actions.

9. Beauty Waits to be Seen

Spli-uhuraret-nichva

Angel name: *Siteher-skrivines*

We mistakenly value external riches, while we overlook internal impoverishment. A life without the depth of contemplations invites loss to be our teacher.

10. The Mystery Beckons

Lesetu-minuvi-ahes

Angel name: *Lisenis-asives*

Many search for the perfect moment, not realizing that the only perfect moment they can ever have is now. The perfection of the moment reveals itself when we find the source of its inspiration.

11. Fluid Mastery

Kresba-stererut-asarat

Angel name: *Rekpahis-nisat*

Those who dare the impossible, are either those who live free from self-reflection or those who, with disciplined determination, silence the voices of their doubts.

12. Enter into What is Before You

Trechbahur-urasvi

Angel name: *Kelsi-aret-munach*

The most dominant need of the heart is the desire for a tribe. The tribe ostracizes the exceptional ones to preserve its mediocre integrity. The exceptional ones seek a tribe by overestimating the mediocre. Let solitude introduce you to the full vastness of your being that your interaction with others may be free of need.

13. Acknowledge Oneness

Stehelanot-uklet-barasvi

Angel name: *Viliherspi-minesh*

It is only those who take the familiar and give it back as wisdom, that receives the world's acclaim. The truly great ones walk the path of the unknown that lies beyond the comfort zone of the masses, where few dare to follow. The rarest of masters live within the unknowable – a path that must be trodden alone.

14. You are Affecting your Environment

Nechpa-resatu-minuvet

Angel name: *Krisatar-brivasu*

Genius does not come from intellectual ability. Intellectual ability comes from genius; that state of being in which mind is silenced and all things effortlessly reveal themselves. Action becomes automatic as we surrender through complete trust.

15. Shun Predictable Conformity

Helshet-akrat-ublabesvi

Angel name: *Nitpers-ereseta*

When overemphasis is placed on doingness, contented peace becomes a stranger to us. Cultivate familiarity with contentment by practicing a few short periods in your day when you come home to the silent company of your being.

16. Mastery through Authenticity

Rukter-plishbahet-nesenut

Angel name: *Vibet-erklavu*

False value is given to the 'what ifs' and 'if onlys' of life. The most valuable asset we have is the fullness of the moment. The circumstances of the moment are truly our gift, even when they are wrapped in seeming adversity. When we, in grateful acknowledgment know this, the adverse wrapping disappears.

17. It is Yourself that You See

Irepu-harasat-mesetvi

Angel name: *Nit-kibelasvi*

The 'what ifs' and 'if onlys' that linger like ghosts in our memories, create the ghost-like or phantom awareness particles that spirit consists of. Spirit is therefore held in place, and in turn, tries to rewrite and control our lives to fulfill these obsolete regrets and desires, causing rebirth cycles of mediocrity.

18. Trust Infallibility

Nankas-pretbarus-araskas

Angel name: *Bilister-unas*

The soul's unfulfilled desires and emotional injuries form the phantom awareness particles of soul. Regrets and unaccomplished achievements form the phantom awareness particles of physicality. Awareness particles, that form the screen upon which life plays out, are the ghosts of the past.

19. Finding the Purpose

Sitru-masanach-bilesta

Angel name: *Kriter-minesvi*

Life, death and ascension as we live it, is not our authentic experience but a phantom reality written by yesterday's regrets. The full embracing of the moment as everything, in trusting surrender, can set us free from the cyclical treadmill of this unreality.

20. New Potential

Karut-nenkles-asusanti

Angel name: *Luvi-erestabi*

Spring does not regret the leaves that fell last autumn, but uses them as fertilizer to reshape the face of the forest with new growth. The events of the past are the fertile soil of the moment. The moment is the inspiration for eternity.

21. Living Beyond Boundaries

Asbaruch-mishbe-haras

Angel name: *Miseret-harsvi*

Only that which resides in a space, can be questioned. Within boundlessness we find only the unexplainable. Because space does not exist, except as an imaginary concept, neither do questions and answers.

22. Harmonious Union

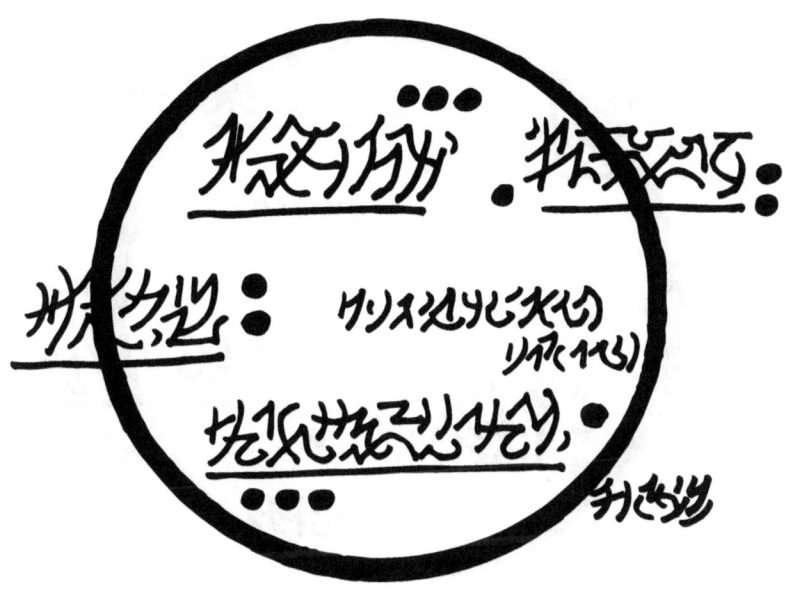

Nesbar-ekvaranot

Angel name: *Kiranus-usi*

The tool used by body, soul and spirit to create a space it can control, is movement, which is linear time. The movement occurs by creating an imaginary imbalance. To do this, the program of the law of compensation is instigated. It keeps movement flowing (which creates a space in which the movement takes place) to rush in to compensate for seeming lack or injustice.

23. Fluidity of Being

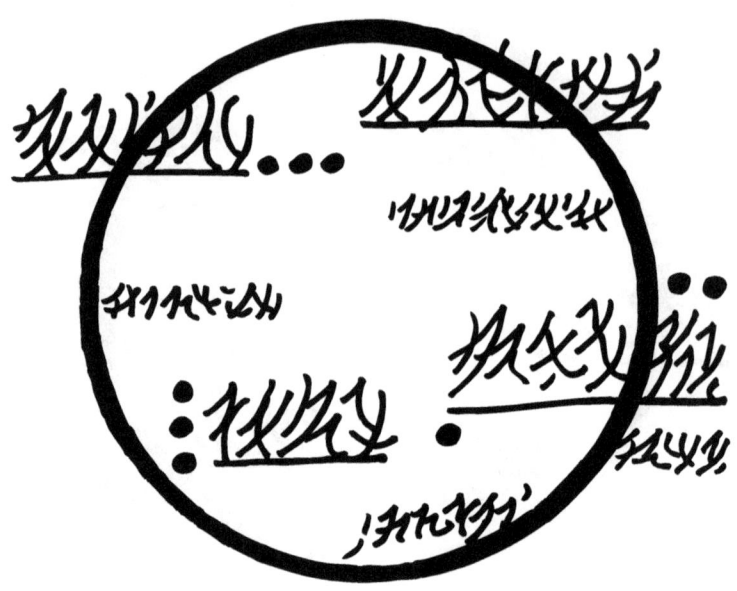

Lu-eresta-misenech-suvavesbi

Angel name: *Plisatar-bravi*

Regrets come not only because of the programmed sense of injustice, but also because of the imagined existence of success or failure. In measuring our success or failure, we use the programmed criteria of the body, soul and spirit. All these criteria presuppose that anything can be amiss or out of place.

24. All is Possible

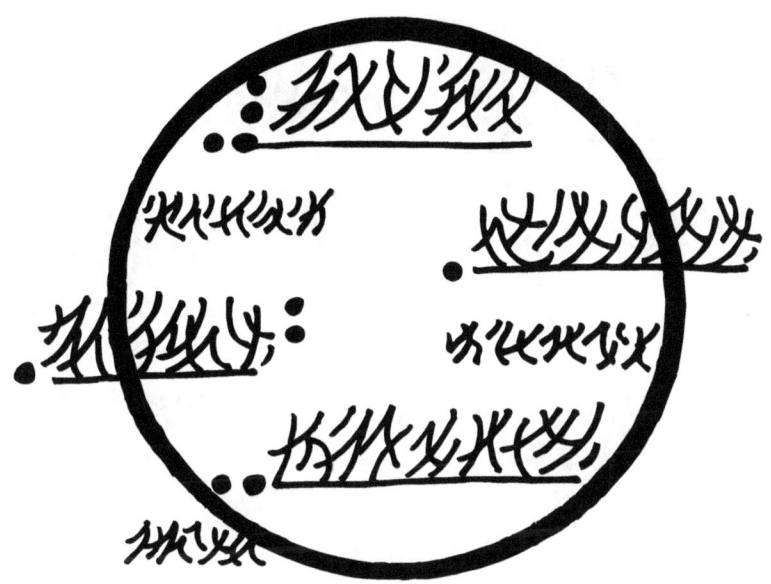

Utanit-stubaha-sikrenut

Angel name: *Vlivarus-bavi*

Spirit controls through guilt. Its program says that you have to justify your existence. The body says that you have to leave the world a better place; you have to leave a beneficial imprint. It creates anger over our apparent insignificance and fear over failure.

25. Releasing Attachments

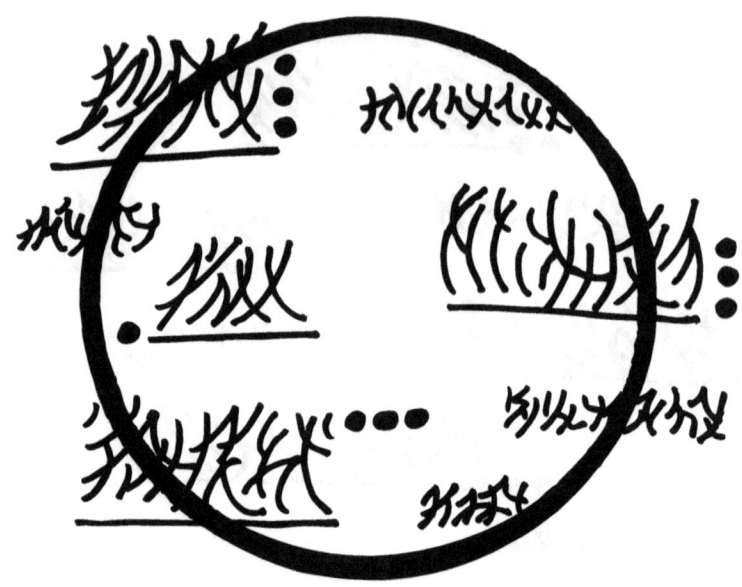

Litrahut-meseba-pispechparut

Angel name: *Kisar-eresvi*

The soul demands that you protect others from the consequences of their folly and the seeming 'imperfection' of the world. It provides us with pain and protectiveness over others' suffering. It prods us to save, help, uplift and fix the ills and pain of the world.

26. Maintaining Sacred Space

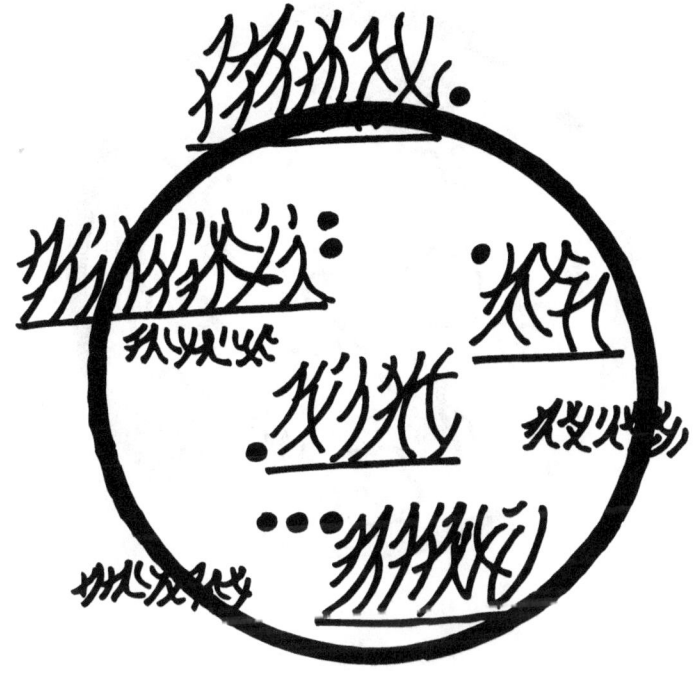

Alsu-nanastra-huret

Angel name: *Michpa-kiveresta*

When we refuse to feel guilt or other negative emotions, by knowing that seeming imperfections are the result of our inability to see the big picture, we have placed our feet on the path of guiltless living without regrets; an existence of freedom to become the opened portal of Infinite expression.

27. Honoring Diversity

Baluk-subata-rechvi

Angel name: *Plisarut-itret*

A moment is an artificial package of time held in place by a regret. Gain its inspiration, dissolve the regret and live instead from the eternity of existence.

28. Seeing the Value of All Parts

Bilshpravek-mestanek-husva

Angel name: *Sihutrer-sklavi*

We have been programmed to believe in beginnings and endings, and furthermore to fear endings as possible cataclysms. Anything that has had a beginning is a ghostly, phantom creation (unreal) – therefore able to be destroyed or terminated. Only the illusion of its existence can disappear when it no longer serves the purpose of Infinite expression.

29. Know Yourself as Divine

Arekvi-sperspa-kruvatur

Angel name: *Pihures-asetra*

The original regret is the illusion that separation can occur within boundless and inseparable oneness. All other regrets are but fractured images of this first regret.

30. Containing All Within

Birata-eklevi-paras

Angel name: *Sihuvatret-misa*

The cosmos is the Eternal Moment held in place by the first regret of separation. The result of feeling separated is the feeling of feeling lost. But you have never left the eternal presence of your being – a current that flows through a boundless ocean.

31. Beginning through Ending

Urchnanes-hisalvaset

Angel name: *Rekpahur-vister*

From a single moment, all others came. From the first regret all others were born. When a contracted feeling of regret within the Infinite created a tone, a geometric shape, a designated space was formed.

32. Freedom's Release

Kersetu-misanet-elestu

Angel name: *Aruvat-pliver*

Many harbor a deep sense of betrayal, manifesting it in their lives again and again. Soul, body and spirit were created as tools of the infinite self, but instead, seized control and put the 'real and eternal' on trial. Opposites and opposition form when we think we need tools. We are the tools and the one who wields them.

33. Dissolving Old Programs

Retrehit-arasve

Angel name: *Kahurastavi-unes*

The building blocks of existence, such as awareness particles, are the ghostly images of past regrets that have been governing life with codes. Codes are programs of expression based on belief systems held in place by the ghosts of the past. Jointly they form matrices and grids.

34. See the Blessings

Huksaret-minetva-pa-ur

Angel name: *Spe-uhururasvi*

Regrets form when we believe that damage can occur due to circumstances. Damage is a result, not a cause. It is an external manifestation of a disempowering attitude. To excuse disrespectful behavior in others because they have been damaged, is to keep them in victimhood.

35. Supportive Environment

Selechsa-plu-uharut

Angel name: *Nesekli-baretvi*

The assertive pursuit of what we want is the overvalued masculine way. Remaining passive while holding the vision of your fulfilled desire, is the feminine principle that goes hand in hand with the masculine. Without applying the feminine principle as well, we do not create the receptive space to receive what we want.

Part III The 144 Precepts of the Higher Life

36. See the Beauty

Serksavis-estavu-revekvi

Angel name: *Kasahur-plista*

To turn opposites into being mutually inspiring rather than mutually hostile, we must trust in the principle that by reaching for the best, we raise the standard and quality of life for all. Denying our own desires creates mediocrity for everyone. Trying to speak up for the unexpressed desires of others, when they themselves do not know what they are, creates eventual hostility from them.

37. Future Promises are Here

Sihet-asava-misavech

Angel name: *Kusinet-ekvabi*

Good and bad are artificial distinctions based on limited perspectives. The understanding of this is the beginning of true humility.

38. Connectedness to the Real

Kereret-mitranus-heset

Angel name: *Itrehut-urat*

Take moments each day to acquaint yourself with the wishes and desires of your heart. Then, with the mastery of discipline, implement them step-by-step. Great decisions are usually momentous, but implementing them is done in small increments.

39. Trust Effortless Knowing

Nanuhit-alsklahet-uras

Angel name: *Tresenach-militret*

Madness is the choice to act contrary to our highest truth. By this definition, most of humanity is in madness. The contradiction of living contrary to one's highest vision is not a logical sequence of events. Do not try to understand the madness of others; unanswerable questions trap awareness and drain resources. Just observe without judgment and without the need to form conclusions.

40. See Behind Form

Rekpa-risetvi-manunas

Angel name: *Brihas-uvaster*

The student asks for what he wants. The master expresses what he wants. The student sees the world around him as a mirror of what he is. The master knows his environment as an expression of himself.

41. Abundant Resources

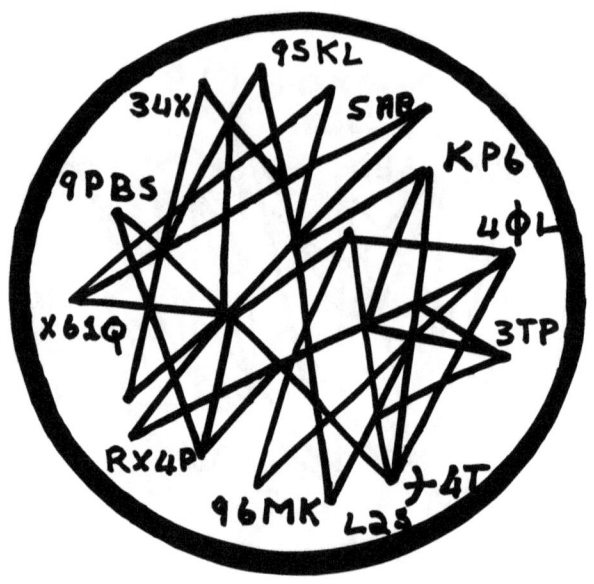

Uluklespa-sitre-ureret

Angel name: *Karus-barasti-uher*

Those who have chosen to disconnect from the matrix to some degree over the years, have been put on trial, judged and condemned by the hordes (the mirrors). It is the mirrors that are on trial. Body, soul and spirit are an example of such mirrors. They are only sustained because the beginningless, endless you has given them validity and credence. If you withdraw it, they cease to exist.

42. Divine Expression

Nanusak-harspi-aret

Angel name: *Mesenit-vilstra*

It is the need for definition and validation that has caused us to keep the unreal in our midst. Through this need, we have been able to be manipulated. The unreal can never define, nor validate the unexplainable vastness of your true being.

43. Direction from the Infinite

Erkpa-blusat-uraspi

Angel name: *Kusunis-plivasta*

There is nothing but the pure self. The matrix is but a condition that obscures it. Yet we have sought answers from it because we have felt lost. The reason for this arises from not understanding that truth is acknowledging that our being is unknowable. Untruth comes from thinking we know.

44. Miracles Through Surrender

Mechpa-hersat-mushelvavi

Angel name: *Arkpahar-kri-es*

Man has felt separated from Source and abandoned. But this is because he has abandoned his real, eternal self to pacify and follow the matrix. His being exists as an inseparable aspect of Source and can never be separated from it – an eternal truth hidden by the matrix.

45. Changing All by Self-Change

Ukru-vespi-manechtu

Angel name: *Kiserut-milistra*

Even though we cannot know ourselves, we can experience the self. Knowing the self through jewels of self-experience lies hidden in the gaps of perception. If you approach life through perception, there are always gaps. True revelations come through experiencing ourselves without mind.

46. Dissolving Density

Heresatvi-nusat-bravi

Angle name: *Pi-uhanar-kivivar*

Accumulated wisdom prevents the fluid dance of existence. Unique and authentic expression is the source of a rich and full existence – not the gathering of another's insights. Gather their inspiration but release the knowledge of yesterday.

47. Peace through Indivisible Oneness

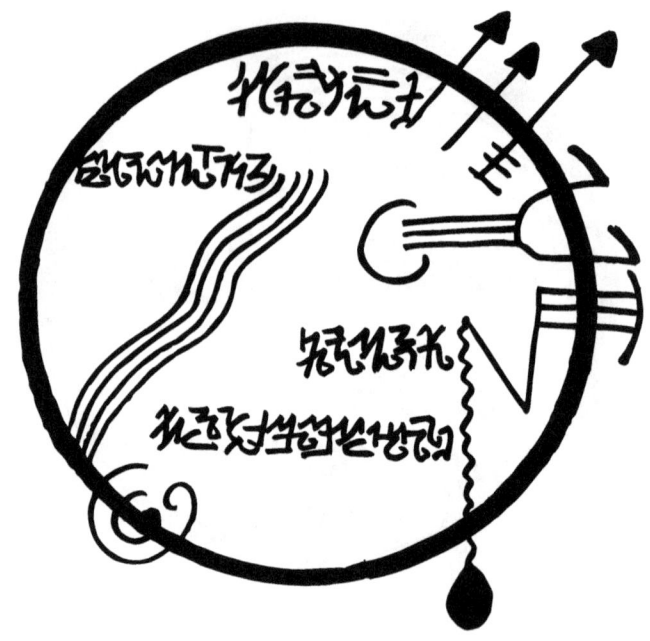

Rusater-menevechvi

Angel name: *Nererek-mikpehur*

The student learns from opposition caused by discontent. The adept lives from the inspiration of circumstances he calls forth through hopeful anticipation. The master knows himself to be the creator and the unfolding play of creations. Whenever parts of the play become uninspiring, he simply withdraws his attention and presence from them. The master lives automatically because the song of eternity unfolding thunders through his being and reveals itself as inevitable action; undeniable and pure.

48. Seeing the Perfection

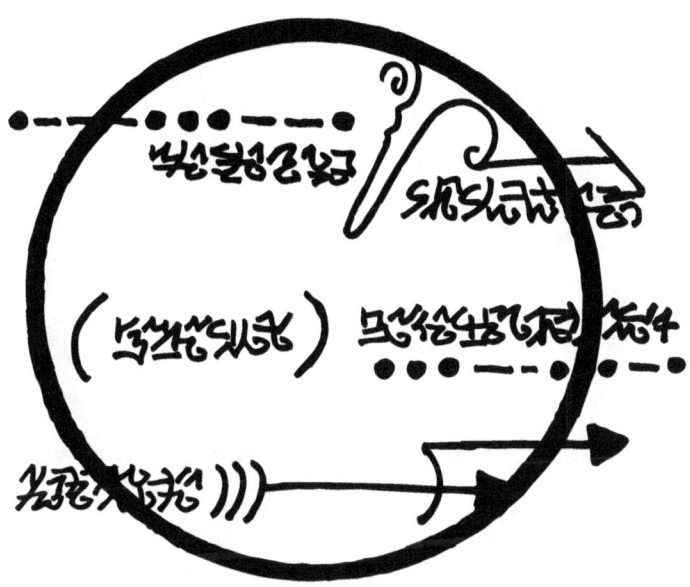

Arsrarasut-ublavespi

Angel name: *Eklet-aranech-stavi*

Time formed when peak experiences of rapture were held onto by the Infinite within Its Being. The entrapment of time keeps us in the circular cage of the past, present and future. This is a treadmill we must step off from, to remember our eternal self as the source of our unique expression. Identity forms from our accumulated story as we travel through time.

49. Dissolving Inner Resistance

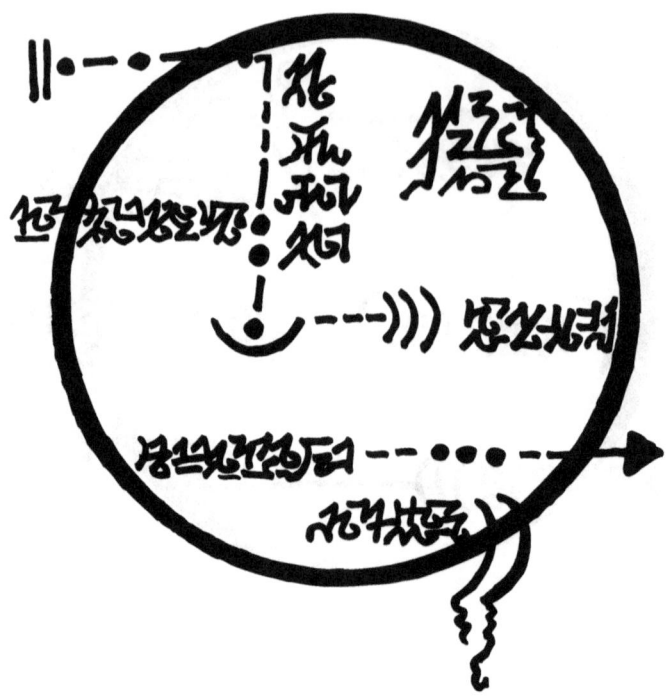

Sechvelvavespi-stiraruch

Angel name: *Stivinus-lihes-stru-arach*

As we travel around and around in cycles of linear time, we create a history which we identify with. The history forms and shapes the body, soul and spirit as vehicles to contain these identities created by the experiences and memories accumulated as we travel through linear time.

50. Letting Go the Need for Order

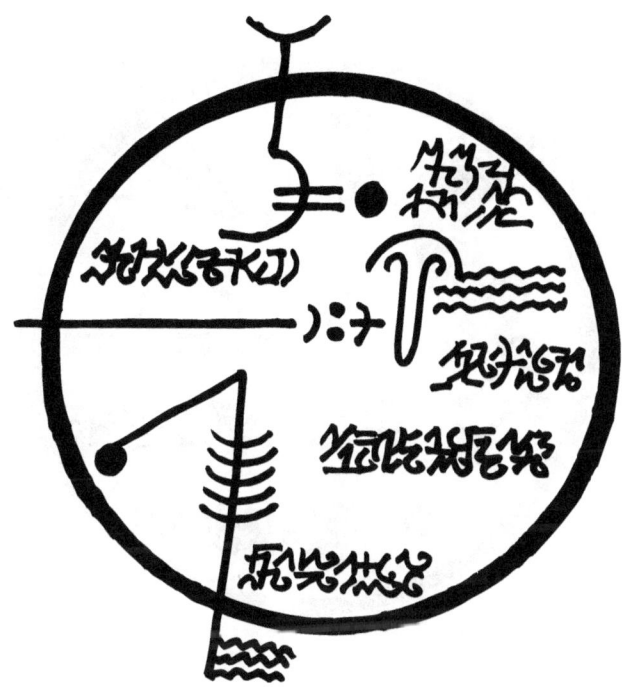

Misach-nesta-velesvi

Angel name: *Nereklut-bisech*

The body, soul and spirit keep us on this treadmill by creating karma through deliberately obscuring vision. They are strengthened (even though they are the result of the identities we accumulate through time and therefore an illusional creation) by: The fictitious belief in the law of compensation that creates karma.

51. Releasing the Need to Understand

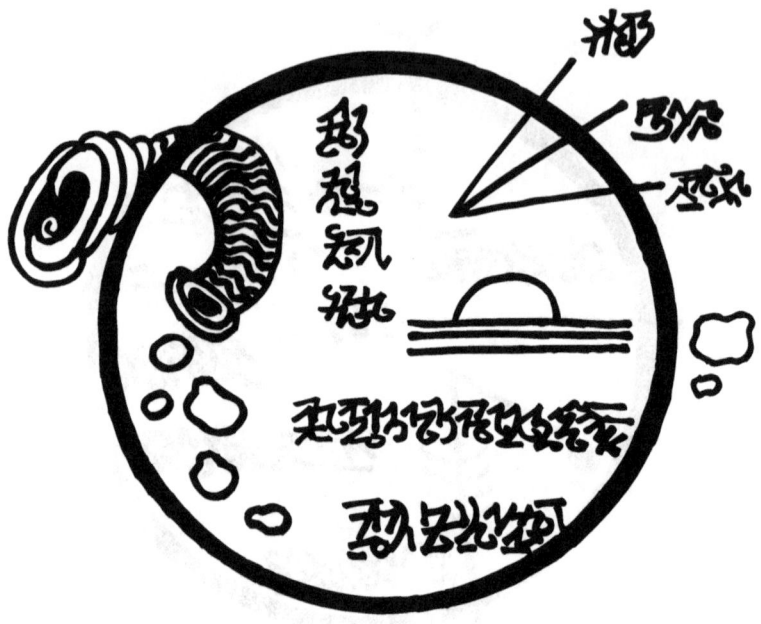

Sekba-herenesvi-urat

Angel name: *Pivi-uhurarestavi*

The use of mind and limited senses as a way of accessing perception, thus allowing parts of existence to be obscured, is the second way of keeping karma in place, to call us back through karma, to the tyranny of body, soul and spirit. The third way is to use guilt and regrets to keep us looking backward, and by compensating for these regrets through planning a 'better' future. This creates linear time and cyclical living.

52. All Knowingness through the Heart

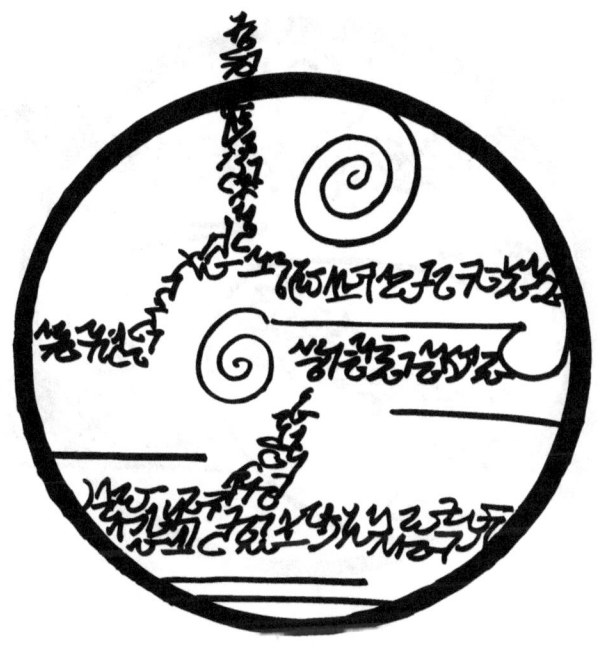

Utre-mananach-savi

Angel name: *Kuris-paravi-huras*

Adversity is the result of polarity – the flow of resources back and forth between poles that have separated. The competitive and adversarial relationship between poles creates an inner war that manifests as adversity without.

Polarity is created by our attitudes in the following way: We strive for certain results in order to control outcome in physicality. This creates the future. We then have an equal and opposite reaction from our soul. It looks backwards by clinging to the past with either sentimentality or self-pity.

53. Seeing from Our Large Identity

Elsahit-pelska-biset

Angel name: *Kersta-ununis*

The opposite desires and reaching, would form a vacuum, as soul and body pull apart, but spirit fills the gap (the gap between the present and the past is what the moment is). Spirit controls the now. It does so through value judgments kept in place by belief systems.

54. Releasing the Illusion of Relationship

Nanska-harasetvi-misat

Angel name: *Karanit-privanus*

It is from the movement forward and backward, that the reference point of the moment is formed; the reference point that tries to remain stationary. The movements into what is to come and what was, create time. Where this movement and reference point take place, space is created.

55. Living Spontaneously

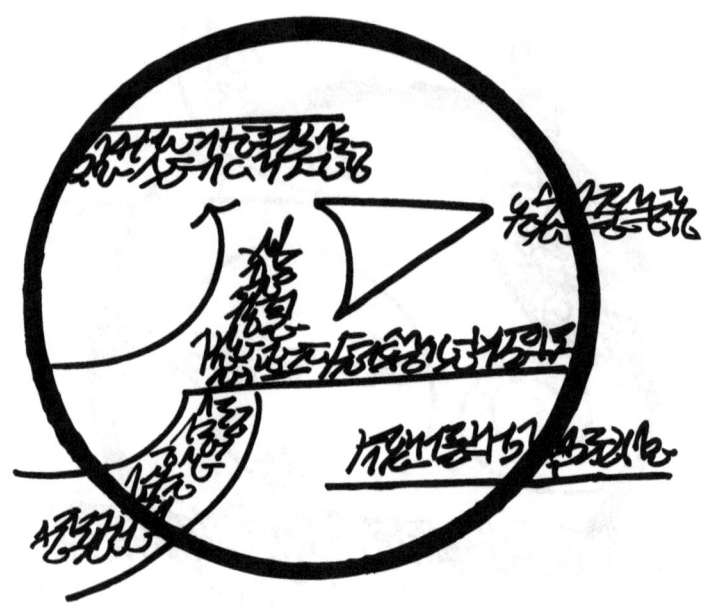

Ratvi-plivabech-urespi

Angel name: *Urusat-prihanas*

The dynamics of the backwards movement (feminine), forwards movement (masculine) and the stationary reference point, creates the two overlapping fields found around the body of a highly evolved being, or can be seen in the Yin/Yang symbol.

The Dynamics of Linear Time

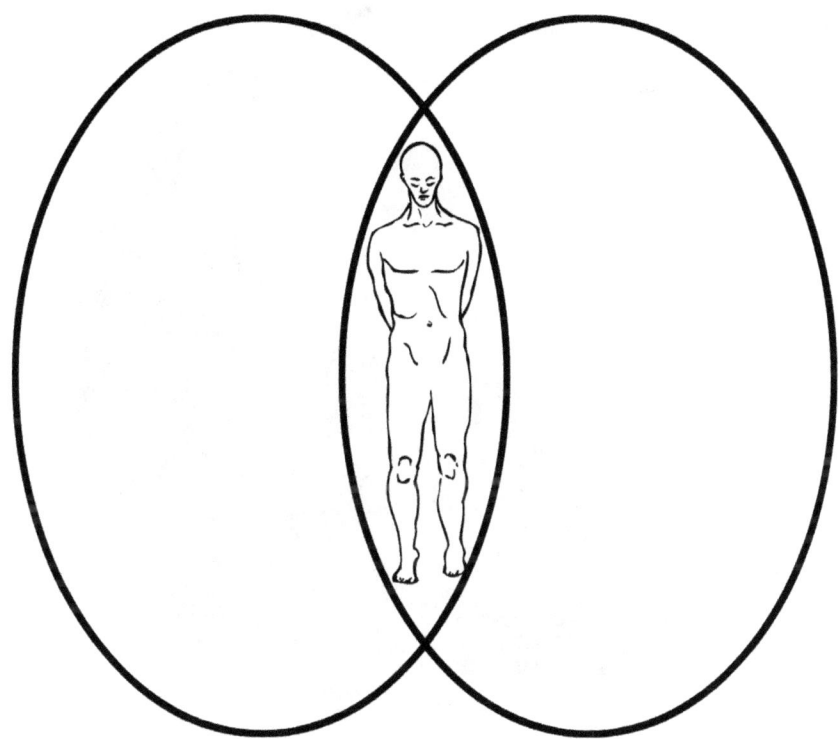

Yin/Yang

56. You Can Excel

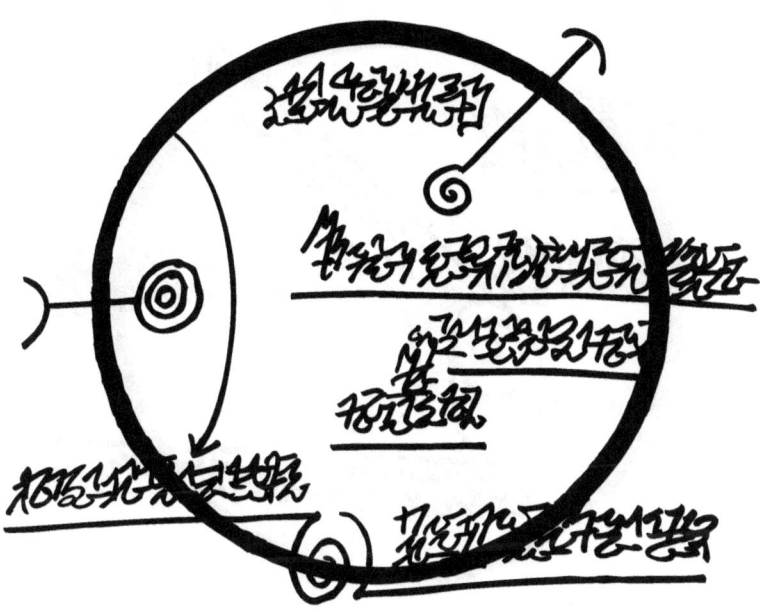

Isiselvatuch-pirasvi

Angel name: *Vlihurat-petrenut*

The feminine (soul) has shallow perception, but depth of experience. The deep experience brings quality to each moment. The masculine has depth of perception, but shallow experiences with less quality.

57. Stimulating Possibilities through Joy

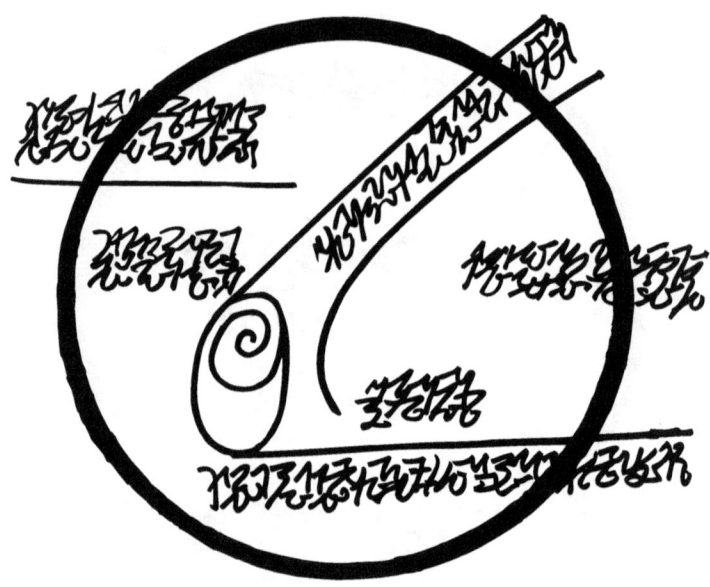

Miselnunavat-hurasvi

Angel name: *Erkpa-plivatur*

When quality is brought into the moments of everyday life, deep insights come effortlessly. What the masculine prizes (insights and perception) come effortlessly when he allows his inner feminine to imbue his life with quality. Beauty, for example, inspires wisdom.

58. Exponential Manifestation

Urspakluvavet-espa

Angel name: *Rinistek-mananur*

To go beyond the matrices and realities formed by the body, soul and spirit, we must fan the flame of our eternal and infinite self. We must recognize the Song of the Infinite singing through us, and step by step learn to live from the deep and endless well-spring of our being. To change the way in which we express and from where we exist, we must not allow the old methods of finding inspiration and joy to be our tools – this would just further tie us into the matrix.

59. Recognizing the Value of Contributions

Nunsarat-helsechvi

Angel name: *Ertreblit-sevava*

The old methods we have used to try and find paradigm shifting excellence and joy include:

- Seeking high points of the past to inspire similar achievements in the present. This puts a ceiling on the achievements of the present, preventing them from rising much beyond past experiences. The past was within the limiting mediocrity of the matrix. Mediocre inspiration produces mediocre results.

Part III The 144 Precepts of the Higher Life

60. Wait for the Right Moment

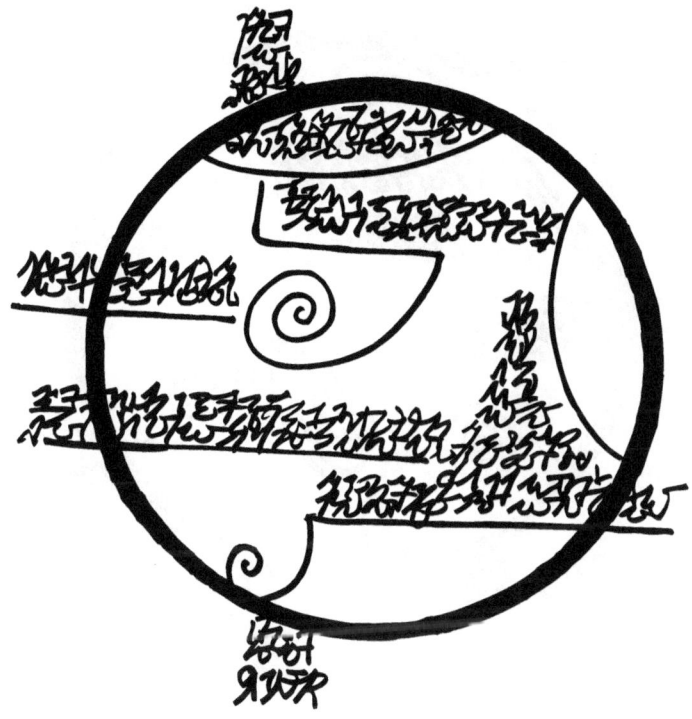

Karspa-birsparus

Angel name: *Nenskara-usitra*

The second obsolete method we use to produce peak experiences of rapture (rapture can arise from the real part of ourselves touching the real part of another) that we hope can fan the flame of our infinite self, is:

- Using external circumstances or events to arouse internal feelings or responses. We seek bliss in the beauty of nature, the association with another and in 'holy' experiences. We create artificial distinctions of worth to produce the illusion of 'holy'. All these external circumstances are but part of the matrix.

61. Dissolving Old Points of View

Elsak-misheter-ubresvi

Angel name: *Pelehistrava-krivet*

We further try and produce peak inner experiences by 'explaining' the unexplainable; by gaining perception. We use light to generate frequency. Both light and frequency are products of the matrix. True beingness transcends both of these and arises only when we are absolutely free of self-reflection and analysis.

62. Knowledge Comes through Stillness

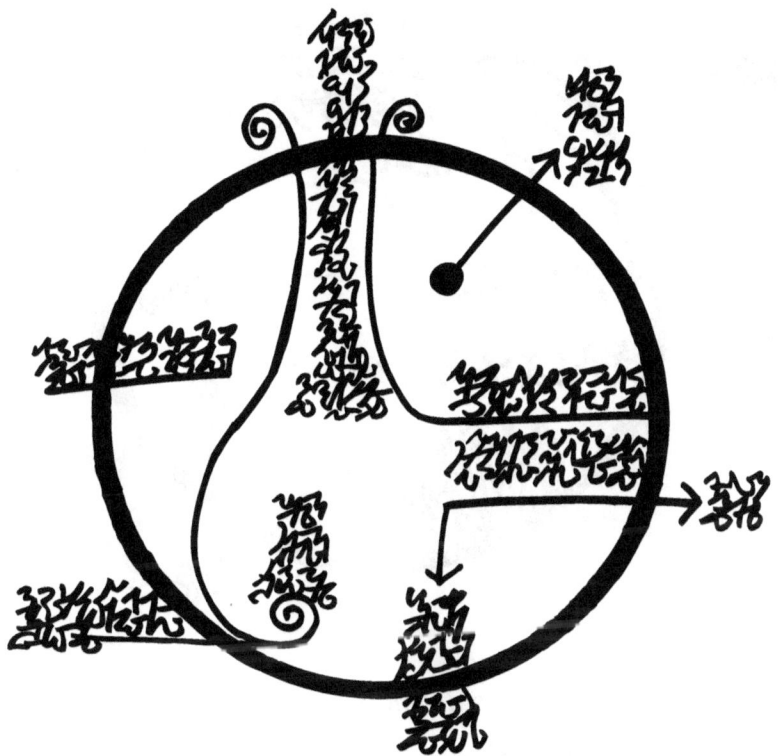

Kavares-hersabich-paret

Angel name: *Urinas-kivinat*

When we continue to seek for the real within the ceiling of the unreal, and by using unreal tools, we become forced to birth beyond it through the birth-pains of deprivation. We receive acute, aware appreciation of aspects of existence by being deprived of them for a long time. The child that spends a long time in a sickbed finds his garden to be a paradise when he can once again play there. The child that can play there all the time is bored with it.

63. Beauty Expressed through Divinity

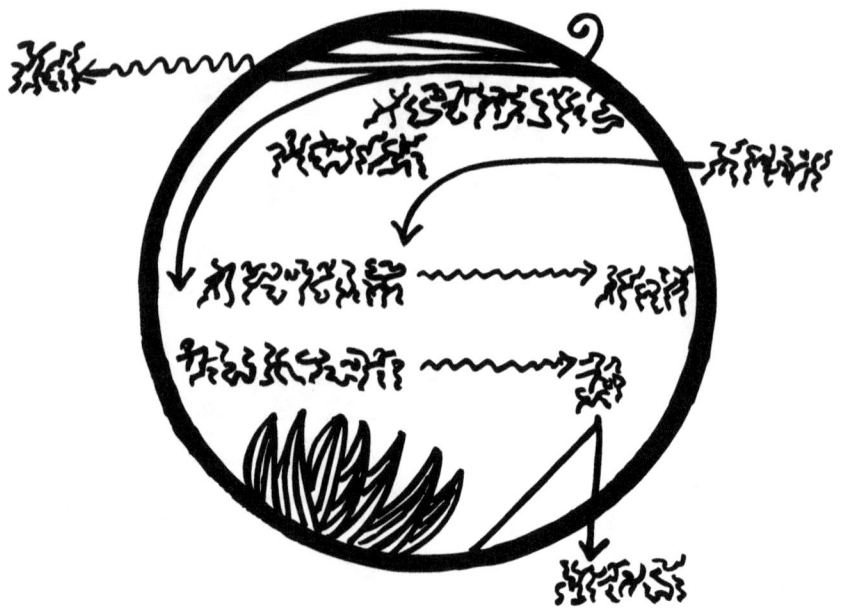

Arasatvi-helsata-unes

Angel name: *Ninaskla-ubisit*

When we live within the matrix, to define it through perception is helpful. It is necessary for the chicken in the egg to know that he is not the confining eggshell. To have the desire to hatch, the perception that there is something more than the shrinking world within his egg, is necessary. But once the hatchling breaks through, he must forsake what he knew and experientially explore the wide world beyond. If he applied his old wisdom in his new reality, he would mistake the dome of the sky as just another eggshell and try to peck at its confinement.

64. See the Beauty of the Journey

Bluhut-naneskar-rektu

Angel name: *Urit-haras-suti*

Practice living from the eternal flame of the infinite self by beingness. Allow yourself just to be in silence (without going into meditation). When thoughts arise, do not engage them, let them rise and fall like the waves of the ocean. Release all programs that beingness is not as valuable as doingness. Jointly they produce superlative results. Release programs that say that beingness is laziness, unless you have an excuse (such as the illusion of old age). Eventually you will be able to experience the unmistakable song of the eternal self even when active.

65. Let go of the Static

Arsvasut-minechtar-bravis

Angels name: *Nanskura-plevi*

Few realize that overworking is counter-productive because:

- We feel out of control when the work becomes the dictator.

- This increases our desire to control, which contracts our perspective as we try to micro-manage the present.

- Increased opposition forms from the increased polarity between doingness and beingness.

66. Assistance from the Unseen

Salvasut-krihaves-atar

Angel name: *Seve-urekvraha*

The contracted perspective creates bodily aches and pains, since they signal what we are not seeing. What we are not seeing increases since contracted perspectives produce myopic vision. The increased work also produces self-pity, which strengthens the soul's pull into the past, increasing the opposition it provides physical life.

67. Assimilating Diverse Perspectives

Nansak-bilshparek

Angel name: *Nutvikla-barut*

We can at first, master feeling the deep peace of infinity by surrendered beingness. Then we can incorporate this true existence into our activity by changing our attitude towards striving for results through labor. The illusion that the little self can write the script of life, must yield to the knowledge that all we can contribute is appreciative perspective. Infinite intent dictates the events in our existence. These can unfold with hardship through resistance, or grace through our effortless interpretation through living beyond body, soul, and spirit.

The Formation of the Matrix

Our attitudes create linear time. By thinking we can hold onto an experience, it creates the past. By thinking we can control outcome, it forms the future.

***

Linear time's three components create the story of our experience as we travel through cycles of time. This forms our identities and illusion of separateness.

***

The history of our travels through time become identities, which become the body, soul and spirit.

***

The body, soul and spirit create matrices that create reflections. These become the unreal realities we get trapped in when we believe them to be real, and allow our body, soul and spirit to define us.

***

Only by knowing that our true 'bodies' are not made of matter, soul and spirit, but something beyond, that has no beginning nor end, can we be free from these illusions.

68. Lightness of Being

Kusunet-varesu-birchpater

Angel name: *Arasu-uter*

Pure sexuality comes from knowing our own wholeness. It desires to give and receive with aware appreciation. When the eternal realness of self touches the eternal realness of another, both are uplifted through rapture. Sexuality that arises from unwholeness and desires to take, is lust. These principles apply to all interactions, even in the relationship we have with the Earth.

Precepts of the
Body, Soul and Spirit

69. Live from Expansion

Letvi-bispa-ararut

Angel name: *Ministech-bitrevar*

The soul is the dream-body that slumbers in the physical body when we are awake and travels into the soul world when we are asleep. Its inhabiting of the body when we are awake, is a parasitical invasion in order to take resources generated by the body. The lower nature of physicality is the result of its lustful occupation of the body. The physical body does not normally have this lustful lower nature.

70. See the Value of the Illusion

Bihars-versanut-ereklar

Angel name: *Eskararut-miretech*

The programmed mind control that the soul, or dream-body, has done to the physical, has made it believe that if the invading occupation of soul ends and soul retreats to its own reality, that the body will die. It makes us revere it through beliefs that 'higher self' will beneficially guide us. But it engineers hardships because we lose resources when we are shocked – which it then absorbs.

71. Recognize Division's Value

Kasunat-palavechvi-birsater

Angel name: *Sitru-huvavespi*

Spirit consists of two levels, and these spirit bodies are also dreambodies, one of higher frequency, the other lower. The lower one occupies the body during sleep when the soul leaves for the soul reality. It creates an inter-dimensional tube torus around the body, imploding and draining resources from the sleeping physical body and its fields. It then moves it into the soul reality by exploding.

72. The Blessing of Destructuring

Velevech-piraret-misetu

Angel name: *Nichtra-blistar*

The higher spirit body occupies the soul in the soul reality while the physical body sleeps. As the lower spirit body steals resources from the physical and passes it into the soul level, the higher spirit body implodes and passes it 'upwards' into its own realms – the spirit realms.

73. Immediate Manifested Change

Ranasuk-misanesvi-arat

Angel name: *Eresatmanus-harspi*

Physicality's reaching and striving for more money, more consciousness etc., comes from its belief that it is deficient (something encouraged by spirit which controls through guilt). The physical feels that there is much it is not expressing and reaches to take from its surroundings to fill the perceived void (this is aggravated by soul's lustful presence in the body).

74. Let All Come to You

Sachva-selvanus-hunes

Angel name: *Karunis-helestra*

The ocean of Infinite existence expresses all the time: it is only appearing as suppressed expression because we have a limited range we can become aware of. Our awareness identifies what we can perceive and categorizes where the gaps in perceptional experience are. These appear as not expressing, even though they are.

75. Living Free from Other's Approval

Kalsanut-istavek-blivasur

Angel name: *Manuvis-ersta*

When awareness categorizes something as 'missing' because it is out of the range of detection, awareness particles rush to fill the gap (like scar tissue filling a wound). They cluster into a matrix and create belief systems that lie like spider webs of programs and fabricated stories. The gap never existed, the awareness particles could not interpret nor understand what was seen or perceived.

76. Finding Deep Enjoyment

Nenparas-hestu-miselvavek

Angel name: *Kuselanut-haruves*

The Infinite, wishing to know Itself, see Itself, and know Its self-expression, created a mirror through having these desires. The mirror consists of awareness particles. Because the Infinite cannot be defined or known or understood, neither the mirror (awareness), nor the interpretation devices (mind and heart) could understand or access any part of the real.

77. Opposition as the Tool for New Birth

Asahik-alesba-nechtararuk

Angel name: *Pisernat-kri-unas*

Because gaps are filled with fabrications and beliefs by awareness, and because nothing of the real could be understood (that which has a beginning cannot understand that which has none), everything we think we know about ourselves is a lie. The mirror thinks aging needs to take place, so it mirrors an aging body to someone, when there is no aging or decay at all in the real body.

78. Confidence in Beneficial Outcomes

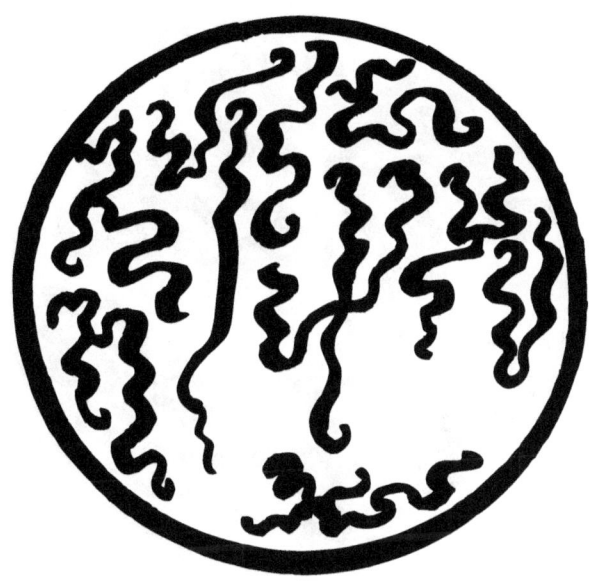

Kuvich-balanustahik-prava

Angel name: *Estravi-rihurutet*

The mirrors of body, soul and mind, have formed to help us do the impossible: know the unknowable. They are tools of self-reflection. The self-reflection of the experiences as we travel through the journey of linear time, strengthens them until they become masks that hide the real's existence.

79. Living in Absolute Truth

Kevelenuchbava-sihartravek

Angel name: *Berit-havahespi*

The mask of the body uses activity and words to affirm itself – valuing activity over beingness to achieve its desired outcome. The mask of soul uses give and take to create polarity of pro-active and receptive. It gives based on wanting to equalize a perceived deficiency. It identifies itself through good deeds and heroism. The mask of spirit uses the mask of worthiness and pretense of being valuable to affirm and strengthen itself. It uses comparison to establish its 'holiness' or desirability.

Part III The 144 Precepts of the Higher Life

80. Humility through Oneness

Lesetuch-bilevechvi-arsnatuk

Angel name: *Kilistar-mananus*

When we live from our indivisible realness, the magic of life is restored. Magic moves out of our range of perception when opposites are at war. Magic is only present when there is innocence. Fear and protectiveness, that arise from adversarial circumstances, destroys innocence. Protectiveness is counter-productive: The minute we try and protect something, we put it at risk.

81. Release the Illusion of Responsibility

Kunat-bribaranesvi-selvenak

Angel name: *Sivinenuset-pelanis*

Trying to break out of the existing paradigm or matrix using peak experiences cannot succeed because there are no peak and low experiences. This illusion comes from value judgments born of limited vision. When the small picture moves, like a wave on the surface of the ocean, we can enjoy its understandable change. When the big picture shifts, we cannot see its eventual resolution and it appears catastrophic from our vantage point.

82. Divine Synchronicity

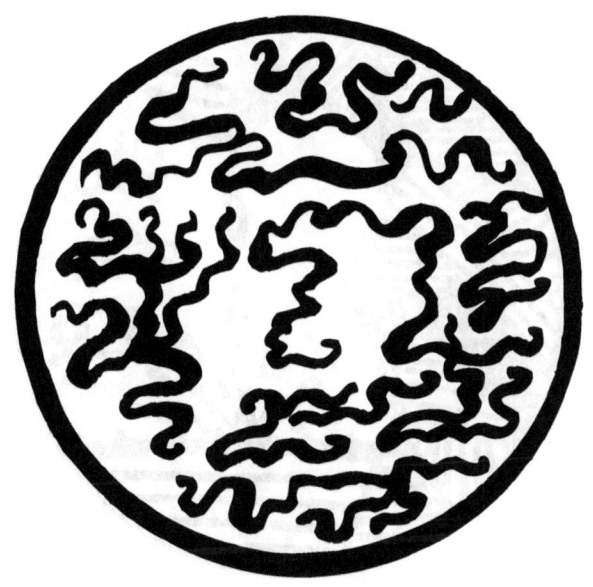

Pruhara-sutvabich

Angel name: *Verenis-harsta*

Because the physical became overactive as it strived for more and more (urged on by soul's presence), it became very electrical. The spin of the disc of life, death and ascension (the treadmill of the matrix) created by the physical, soul and spirit, changed rotation. The more magnetic, frequency-based reality spun clockwise. The more electrical, light-based reality, created by physicality's increased electricity, spun the disc in the opposite, counter-clockwise direction.

83. See What is Obscured behind the Obvious

Letrebistevek-vivachvahur

Angel name: *Urunat-upestriva*

The way a power-surge erases memory (held by the magnetic components) from a computer; memory began to be erased from the realms of soul and spirit. They created a conspiracy to drain the resources from the physical by their dream-bodies invading it. This would have depleted it, except for the fact that the physical reality started spinning faster and faster in a counter-clockwise manner from its hyperactivity. A counter-clockwise rotation forms a centripetal force that pulls in resources inter-dimensionally. It began draining soul and spirit realms.

84. Divine Timing

Kresbahut-misevelenech-vihar

Angel name: *Herenit-skeleva*

How to live beyond the games of masks and war begins by dissolving these dream-bodies (the physical is a lucid dream-body). This is done by:

- Intending that as we fall asleep, we dissolve into our eternal being's indescribable rest.

85. Flawless Expression

Rektavur-sitrehelechvi

Angel name: *Sta-ubit-viberech*

To live from the flame of our infinite, indivisible self:

- Refuse to live the programmed existence of masks, identities and belief systems.

- Embrace the unknowable nature of all.

- At first in passive silence, then in activity, allow the silent song of your eternal self, to be felt and known by you, that your automatic actions be inevitable.

86. Patience through Trust

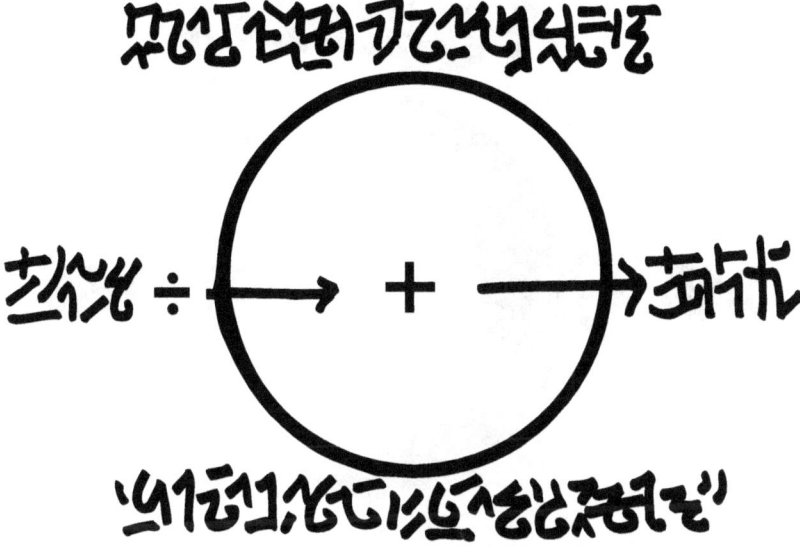

Karsu-ninasvur

Angel name: *Nanusubit-klevivas*

The cosmos is a self-generating, free-energy device that has tried to imitate endlessness of motion. It fears ending, but because it had a beginning itself, it has to keep engineering ways to keep its sub-created reality going.

87. Your Actions Impact the Many

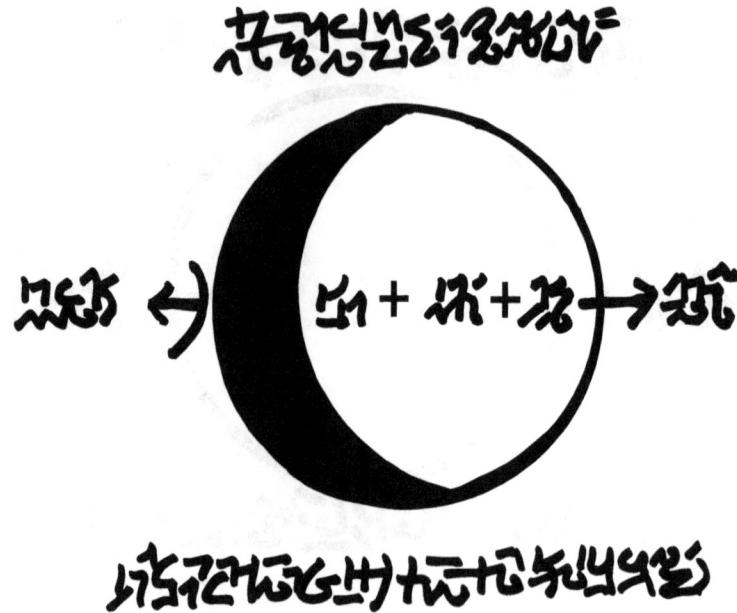

Bilshpa-mechpasur

Angel name: *Skeresut-virstahit*

The moment is the window into eternity; the place where opposites meet and we can remember oneness. It is the still reference point between two opposing forces that holds structure together.

88. Do Not React — Stay in the Stillness

Ratvi-pelech-vibrespi

Angel name: *Kavanit-trivanus*

The moment is a parcel of linear time. Wherever there is time, there is space. The parcel of time known as the moment, is a space consisting of a tube torus. The hole of the tube torus can provide a window into eternity if we release past regrets which accumulate there as karma.

89. Fulfillment Lies in Grateful Awareness

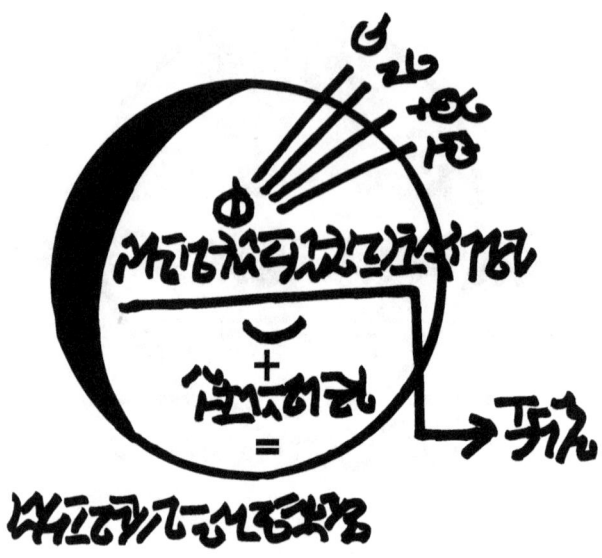

Kesevesbahur-alaskrelasvi

Angel name: *Elsenis-prihespa-ur*

The perfect moment is when the contribution we make to living the moment, creates alchemy that allows the moment to become an opened portal of Infinite intent. This releases the power inherent in the moment.

90. Beneficial Outcomes

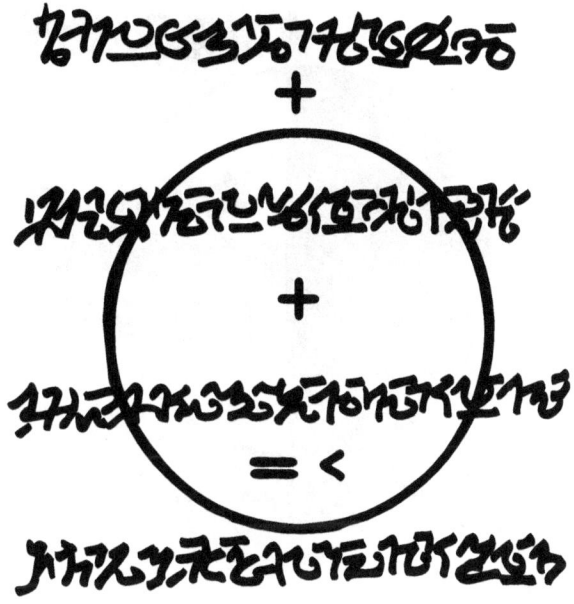

Astanoch-miset-valasvi

Angel name: *Travanit-plisher*

The pranic tube of the body is the center of the tube torus around the body. When we live from our still point, the center of the pranic tube, in the moment (which can be called the still point of time), our influence on our environment becomes powerful. (See illustration of Pranic Tube page 173.)

91. Trust in the Benevolence of Life

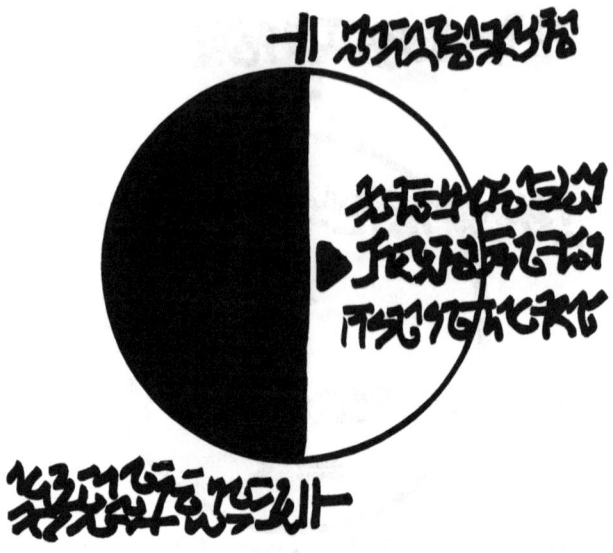

Akbar-siklahut-asatar

Angel name: *Nekurat-kerstevit*

If we approach the moment without agenda it becomes the window into eternity. The cosmos itself is the 'eternal' moment that is the reference point through which existence seeks a deeper understanding of its meaning.

How the Moments are Formed
(A diagram of the Wheels of Physical, Soul and Spirit Realities)

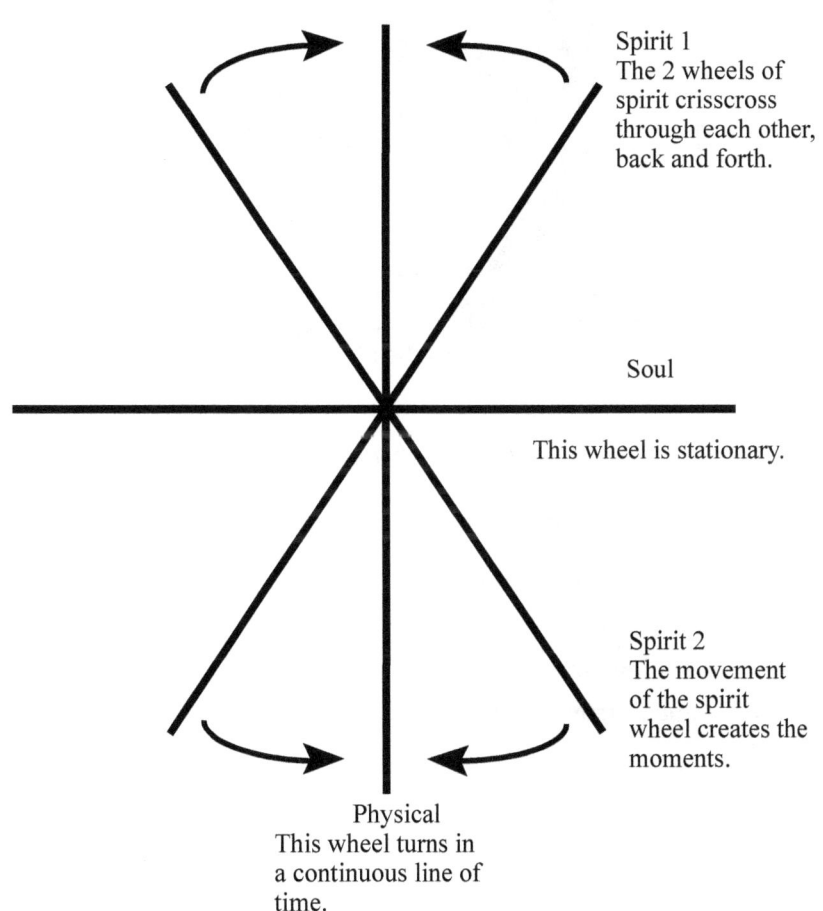

92. Solitude Brings Greatness

Aruk-mesh-halasvi

Angel name: *Sunach-elsetmavi*

The moments are formed by the back and forth movements of the two planes of spirit as they move through each other in a scissors-like movement, slicing the line of linear time into sections. This forms inner or psychological time and the time of our external environment.

93. Move beyond the Familiar

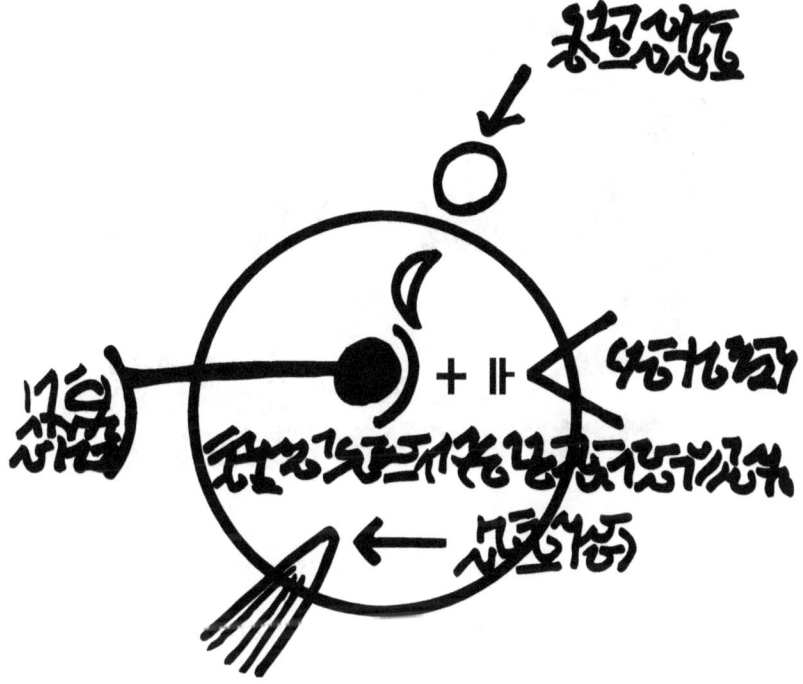

Libranut-utre-selvasvi

Angel name: *Arlavis-treksanut*

There is no past and no future. Thus all is happening now. There is therefore only one moment in existence and we are exploring different aspects of the same moment.

94. Move Out of Stagnation

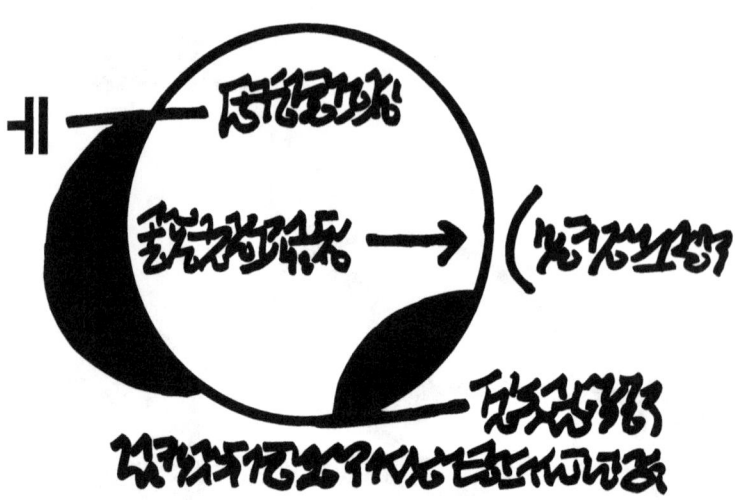

Kerenech-pliherastur

Angel name: *Mivabach-ruvetvaset*

The moment is a temporary perspective of the Infinite. When a moment is deeply lived, it becomes fulfilled. It is then that we know there never was any time at all. Examine the illusions of existence but do not solidify and empower them by trying to 'fix' them.

95. Innocent Discovery

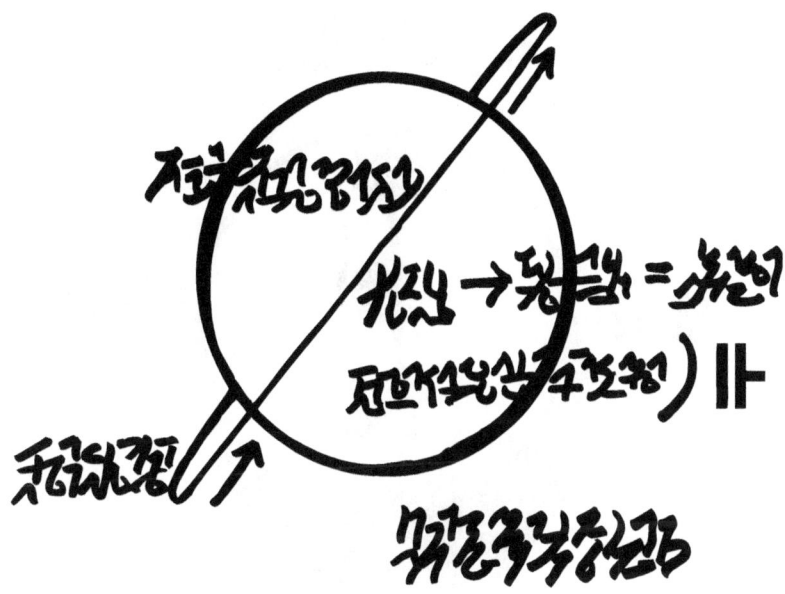

Kasur-nenas-selavi

Angel name: *Sivihet-privehestravi*

The original 8 cells from which the fetus forms, are the only cells of the body that never renew themselves. Spirit programs these cells to write in how it wants you to live your life so that it can control physicality. The 8 cells' programs form the illusions of the 4 stages of dreaming and the 4 stages of awakening.

96. Release All Preconceived Labels

Palesh-usaklut-virsahit

Angel name: *Karunat-setvavi*

The 8 cells have 18 illusions each. The 144 precepts of the Hadji-ka contain the insights necessary to release these programmed illusions and set physical life free from the controlling dictatorship of spirit. The programs in these cells have controlled both inner and outer space through the alpha chakra (magenta), one hand's length below the base of the spine. The 144 Hadji-ka wheels embody the pure frequencies of the 8 cells.

Part III The 144 Precepts of the Higher Life

Precepts of the Mysteries of Existence

97. Broaden the Focus

Krisanut-arsta-biharanut

Angel name: *Kliplenus-privavi*

Charech setve akvet enuskava. Briset ekleve huraset misku-uvanet etreklasvi archprava.
In my beingness I dwelled. It was then the first question arose.

Karsanik herstu arachve sihuvet?
Is there anything I am not?

Pelsparanuk hersut arekvatu, brisparanut keret nasnatu.
Thus space arose also, formed from a question and answer.

98. Let Infinite Compassion Flow

Alech-visarut-pruva

Angel name: *Arunit-peretvavi*

Kranatnuk birchpahur sevet ares aresta. Karus este michpahur nanastu pares hirsvata.

This created the first division. A space containing the known was established.

Kanus helsech brat paravi sesatvi hurasta minech, klavesh ersach vibras bravi-ananess.

This imaginary distinction formed the first directions; they were that of within and without.

99. Release the Ties of Love

Nansuk-hisva-erestur

Angel name: *Isech-melevechvi*

Ka-ashurat mesanech stri-hu arak-klasaret misavech viresta michpahur senatvi aras kle virspavet uvraves.

In the attempt to gather the known, the stories of experience were stored in the vehicles of the body, soul and spirit.

100. Dissolve Egocentricity

Biraset-manech-vechvi

Angel name *Ritva-brivarutbavi*

Klesha misatu ninech aras satsavi heres uratvi mespata stahilavik nenechta.

Gathered information is what light is, and with frequency, it forms the matrix.

*Itrehut minasat esekle birech vilesvit arasva hiresat.
Sehut atra bishenet.*

Forever questions and answers recede like the horizon.
Knowledge is a window.

Ukrus vraba sebehetvi nisechvi arsta mekret usanech

The tools of gathering and labeling the perceptions were formed.

101. Independent Assessment of Truth

Kalsbanaruk-harsatu

Angel name: *Kavanu-hatvi*

Nesklet suvravach sivech mishap heret urasta. Sekenetvi ursat pihirach nesba-uranet sklavanis praha.

These became denser as experience was identified. Classification began to affirm the solidity of matter.

Nestarek nachstu sebek herenet uklatvi nasba ereklut spa-urat hersu vilesvi.

The dividing for the sake of giving the impression that anything can be known, continued.

102. Genius through No Mind

Ublech-perenutvi

Angel name: *Isabit-hersat*

Kusba estehur nanek erespavi nanachvi harsta. Sebehechvi nech suvabit.

The Infinite One began to trap Itself in Its own imaginings. It saw Its divisions as real.

Nachvi suvech misa belestu kravis. Rekta birat marna vravi sparet aklat priharas vravi.

Knowledge seemed superior to Its own inability to know. It deferred to the tools It had made.

Precepts of the Embodiment of the Infinite

103. Release Yesterday's Truth

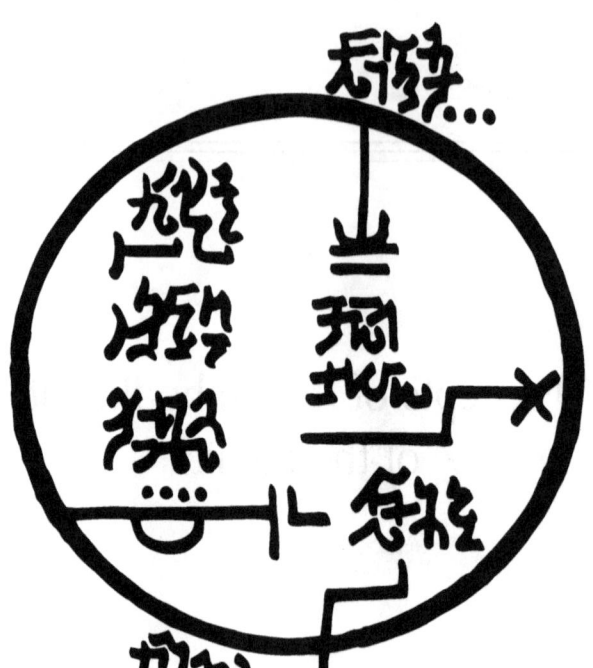

Hesetrech-mishalnavet

Angel name: *Li-esetret-barus*

When knowledge is stored, individuations form. It is not the end of a thread, but the beginning of a never-ending one. Body, soul and spirit were originally perspectives for the Infinite to examine Its own Being from different vantage points. They began to identify with their experiential knowledge and became seen as real aspects of the Infinite Self.

104. Immaculate Unfoldment

Plibararesvi-ustra

Angel name: *Ninklet-sikluhet*

The belief in an existence of boundaries gave the impression that there was individual ability to manipulate outcome. The illusion of self-volition formed from limited perspectives, and more questions are formed when there are parts of existence we cannot see.

105. See the Perfection of Delays

Archba-spiheladonk

Angel name: *Usanus-usabavi*

The Embodiment of the Infinite became unseen as the Source of the existence of the individuations and they misunderstood the original intent of their existence: as a means of Self-exploration. The body made its own tools of exploration: the senses, which affirmed the seeming solidity of matter.

106. Graceful Surrender to Change

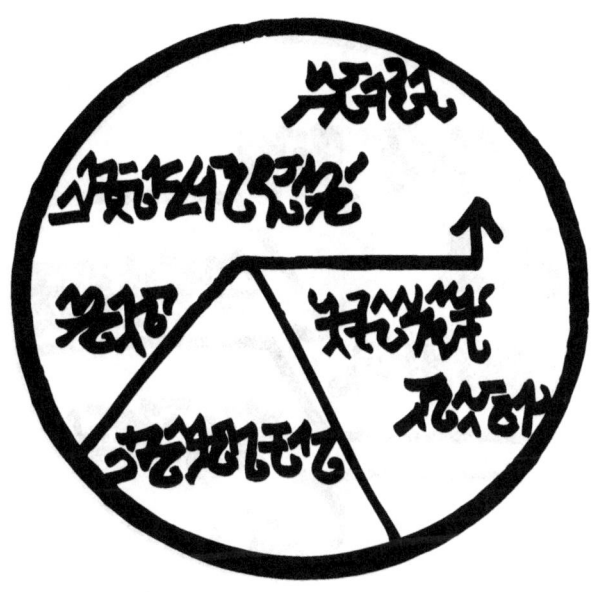

Kresba-retva-uklus

Angel name: *Kerut-eklavi*

No valid question exists, since it stems from limited vision and can only create a limited answer. A limited answer begets another question and in addition, the answer increases the obscured vision by creating the illusion that we know. In this way, perspective became more and more contracted, as more questions arose.

107. There are No Gains or Losses

Velspa-retklat-spirarus

Angel name: *Mistech-ritbahur*

Illusion increased as more gaps in perception arose, since illusion is a story that fills in the gaps; that which from our limited perspective we cannot know. Mind deduces and concludes, to try and organize the unknown into the known. It does this with programs of illusions.

108. Release Expectations

Nuchpera-privesvi

Angel name: *Raksut-nesvi*

The unanswerable question the Infinite asked was: "Is there something beyond My existence?" Because it was unanswerable, the Infinite paused in Its expression to examine the first example of the 'unknowable'. The unknowable does not really exist; it is just the result of an impossible question. But in Its pausing, It became an observer and an illusional reality sprang up as an 'opposite' – it became the observed.

109. Release the Need to Save Others

Livaset-nenklet-pretprahur

Angel name: *Seleba-husur*

An observer is only that because it has stopped self-expression and is vicariously living through the observed. Self-abandonment strengthens the direction of without, and causes addiction to something in the 'outer' reality. A self-sovereign existence expresses and observes at the same time.

110. Enjoy the Adventure of Life

Arsavech-hestrevi-esetar

Angel name: *Niste-krevene*

The Embodiment of the Infinite is called thus because It has interacted 'within' the matrix with the beings within the dream. The Embodiment of the Infinite never has had a body, soul or spirit, the way the individuations of the dream have.

111. Break Free from the Tribe

Halsbakbarut-kisevech

Angel name: *Nurat-nisparu*

The Infinite's Embodiment appears the same as humanity because one can only detect at the level of one's expression. Furthermore, humanity has senses designed to perceive at matter, soul and spirit levels only – illusions the Infinite's Embodiment does not consist of. Only the deeper, eternal sensory capacities can perceive a fraction of the Infinite's glory.

112. Challenge Conventional Wisdom

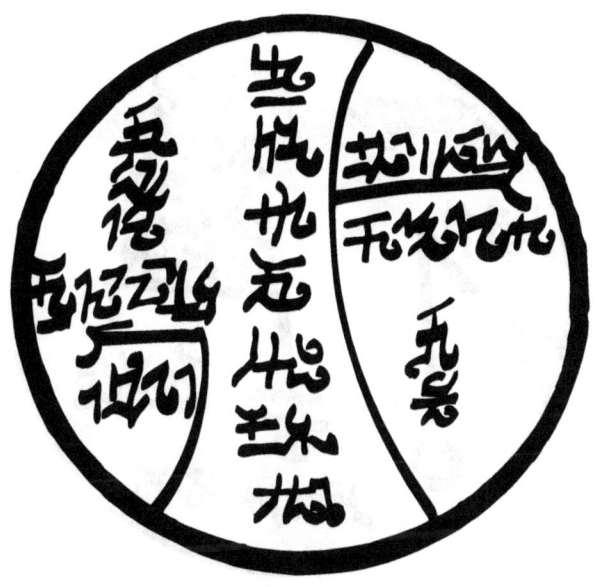

Ukrut-nensavachvi-pruhes

Angel name: *Kutre-virebit*

Inner sensory capacities are awakened by overcoming the addiction to emotion. In the mesh of light and frequency, the substance of the dream – emotion – creates an indentation, like a thumb impression in clay. A negative emotion creates indentation that is filled with distorted light. This forms sub-creations of distortion in our lives because light plus frequency shapes our environment.

113. Do Not Pacify Illusion

Asut-vilasklar-brivabet

Angel name: *Vister-arunasvi*

With matter and frequency, opposites repel and similar matter and frequency attract. With light and frequency opposites attract. It is for this reason that painful or difficult circumstances and emotions yield perception. The distorted light in the indentation of negative emotions (which is opposition) attracts light consisting of accessed information, to enhance perception.

114. Acknowledge Accomplishment

Kasanut-akset-viselvi

Angel name: *Kersta-ertebit*

Positive emotions fill the indentation in the mesh of the disc of life with light. Light is accessed information of the stories of body, soul and spirit. These positive emotions harbor the information of previous matrices and therefore strengthen the matrix. There are deep movements of feeling beyond emotions, that arise from our eternal existence, that open infinite capacities.

115. See the Answer in Others

Varablut-skrubahur-ninasvu

Angel name: *Kirsta-mananush*

Because opposite light attracts, the positive emotions and light attract opposites that bring hardship. Furthermore, the programs of accessed light as belief systems, create stuck and stagnant areas on the disc of the light, that call forth forced change in the form of opposition. It can therefore be said that all emotion either is pain or calls forth pain.

116. Dissolving Belief Systems of Failure

Kisplet-praternot-huvesvi

Angel name: *Sihet-eklevirebit*

We either encounter these opposites in this life, or we manage to avoid them, and then have to encounter them when we come around the disc of life to the same place again. If we pay the price in this life, it is called the law of compensation. If we pay it in another life it is called karma. Forsaking the illusion of opposites is the only way out.

117. Living a Life of No Opposites

Lachbarut-nunasetvi-velanut

Angel name: *Lasanir-mitrevi*

As we travel around the disc of life and encounter the mesh that is created by memories imprinted by emotion, how do we avoid the opposition of a life within opposites? By having a frequency so different from anything else, that we create a different reality around us. This pocket of another reality allows the light to bend around us – a similar principle to stealth technology.

118. Harmony through Shadow

Asenut-vilevet-prahut

Angel name: *Runabit-ekla*

The only way we can have an entirely different frequency from anything else that exists within individuated life, is to fully express the unique frequency we each possess: the Song of the Eternal Self. When it is sung in each moment, life cannot stick to us nor bring opposition.

119. Conjuring Truth

Sekbarut-arsta-arekvi

Angel name: *Viriste-araspavi*

Opposition occurs when we express one part of life, to the exclusion of its opposite. The uniqueness of the individuals' song has no opposite, just the complement of others' individual songs. The violin section of an orchestra is complemented by the wind instruments, rather than being their opposite.

120. Creating Pleasant Dreams

Lasenut-skribahur

Angel name: *Rekta-vibrespi*

It will evoke strong feelings from others when we stir their authentic song by expressing ours, one way or the other. But it will not matter since you will be 'untouchable' by sticky emotions, living in the world but not of it.

121. Becoming Aware of Origins of Actions

Mesenech-kri-huvanesvi

Angel name: *Karut-kanitpavi*

The way to sing the Song of Self is to strengthen it through appreciation of as much as you can find each moment to be glad about. All we can experience is an aspect of the self. As we appreciate as many things as possible, we accentuate their expression within – like notes that play within so that our song can express.

122. Purified Feelings as Guidance

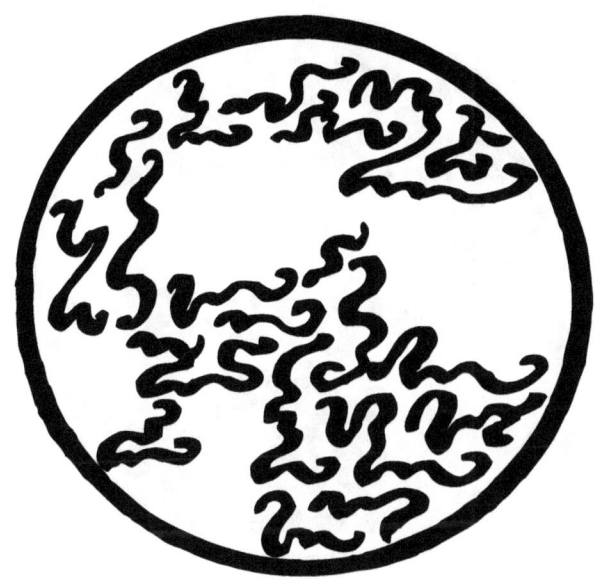

Plubis-ararast-nesatu

Angel name: *Brispe-huretvi*

We attract the pockets of light that lie on the disc or wheel of life as programmed belief systems, when we do not express the Song of the Self. They attract opposition in turn, because the cosmos conspires to break up stagnation. The reason we attract them is that when we are not home for ourselves by expressing our individual song, we yearn for a 'home'. The belief systems promise us a home in the form of the illusion of security, predictability, and stability. We therefore attract these false substitutes for true expression through appreciation. Having a poetic or artistic perspective, assists in cultivating appreciation in order to awaken the Song of the Self.

123. Freedom from Destiny's Callings

Raktu-pri-asbahuch

Angel name: *Michpe-suvahet*

The use of tools in our existence, such as body, soul and spirit, creates duality by creating a relationship between the one who wields the tool and the tool itself. It is for this reason that the use of tools manifests opposition – a result of having opposites.

124. Change of Pace

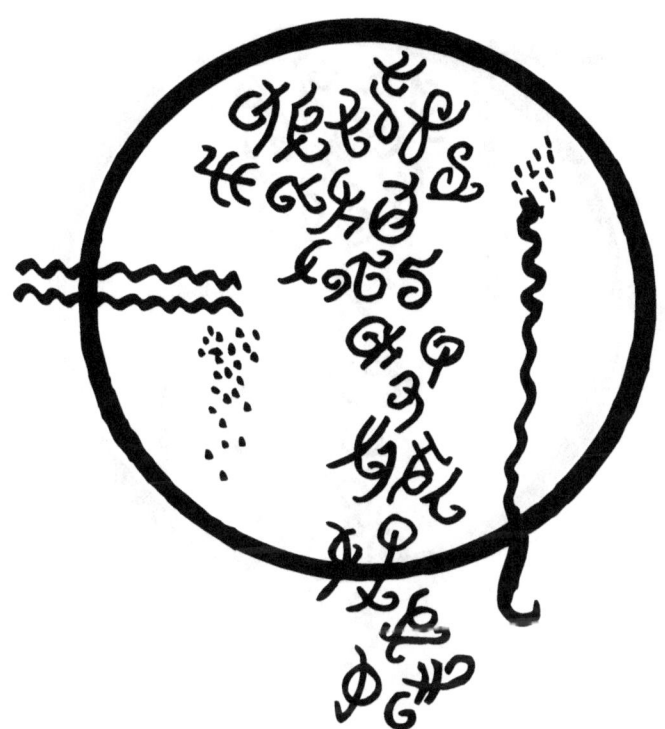

Menesekva-visetar

Angel name: *Arknahur-uklet*

The tools are at first seen as being essential – the way a chicken inside an egg depends on the eggshell to provide the shelter in which he can develop. The second stage of the use of tools sees tools as illusions but still makes use of them for certain purposes. In the third stage, tools are no longer needed during self-expression.

125. Becoming Self-Referring for Approval

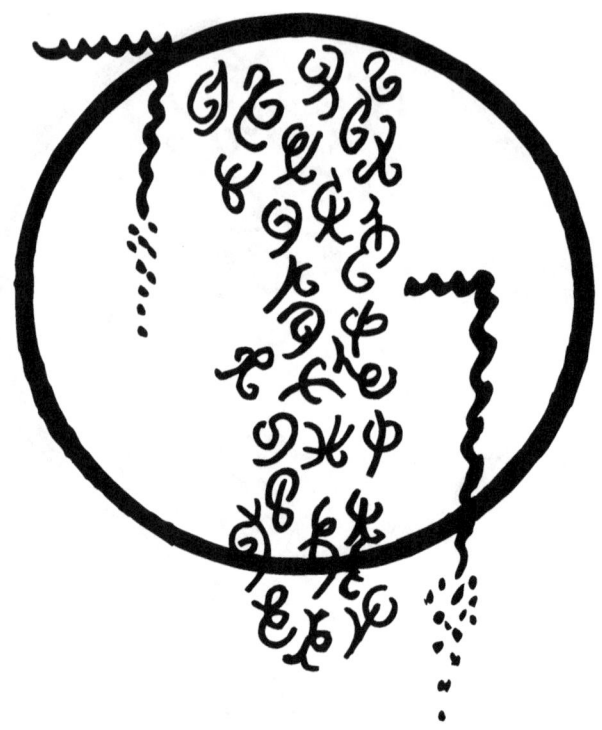

Lihar-nanenustrava

Angel name: *Krasanut-plihes*

During the second stage, tools are used as indicators and catalysts to stimulate specific facets of expression of our eternal beings' qualities. A headache can be treated as follows: A headache pill is clearly seen as an illusion; an unreal tool that cannot possibly affect the real. But the person with the headache takes it to stimulate the expression within that the tool represents 'without'. It becomes an illusional catalyst to guide and awaken inner expression of the eternal self.

126. Speak from the Heart

Pribas-klusavar-archbi

Angel name: *Nanaklu-bruvabi*

There are 12 tones to sing within your being and its expression, to replace the distorted emotions of guilt and blame:

Exuberant beauty	Interdimensional presence
Luxurious passion	Unencumbered enthusiasm
Fluid change	Revitalized existence
Joyous vibration	Expressing the heart-song
Innocent effervescence	Shape-shifting cosmic play
Eternal rejuvenation	Unfolding sensual refinement

127. Listen with Detachment

Nesherasvi-ukretar

Angel name: *Krasatur-uras*

When the tones to dispel guilt are all lived and expressed, they birth a thirteenth quality: Coming home to the silence between the particles.

True eternal existence is not found in the building blocks of life; in the subatomic particles. It is in the indescribable presence of no electromagnetic particles.

128. The Living Voice of the One Life

Aravesvi-hechbararut

Angel name: *Irkpahur-mines*

The deepest core cause of shame is the feeling that we should know why we are in the matrix, how to live beyond it and what the purpose of our existence is. We feel we are somehow inadequate in the game of life and strive to justify our existence. We also gather the best wisdom of those who have gone before but it provides no answers to these questions.

129. Relinquishing the Need to Speak

Vasvanes-bisatut

Angel name: *Sitrahet-vibresvi*

We are learning the use of tools, like time and space and body, soul and spirit, as though we do not know why they have been created. The matrix is like a bucket in the ocean. You are a current within its vastness, present in both the ocean and the bucket. But the ocean has no retention of memory. Your real presence in the bucket is likewise unable to have any memory. This real part of you within the matrix is like someone with amnesia.

130. Responding with the Power of Silence

Leksarut-mespa

Angel name: *Atrabit-splihech*

The cosmic matrix is like a single cell held in place by a desire to know itself. Only within the matrix can memory be held within the building blocks of life, thus only here can anything register as something we know. The cosmos is therefore a tool of self-examination.

131. The Poise of Purity

Suknet-salesach-vavi

Angel name: *Kisbarut-erstavi*

The matrix, or world around us, is like a mirror, and therefore reflects backward images. In doing so, it confronted us for the first time with the concept that there is something we are not – the origin of duality – since it created the illusion that something other than ourselves exists.

132. Listen to the Silent Whispers

Prubares-misetu-havanes

Angel name: *Erstrahut-salvavi*

The backwards reflection of our environment, makes the outer mirrors an unreliable tool of self-observation. Because it is opposite, the external environment provides opposition: the origin of conflict. A second set of mirrors is needed to reverse the backward images once again, in order to have an accurate reflection.

133. Listen behind the Apparent

Nerut-halskla-velavi

Angel name: *Ektra-barasut*

The physical body's external mirrors are the soul and two layers of spirit. The second set of mirrors is found within our inner space; they also represent soul and spirit. Inner mirrors are activated by vibrant, heartfelt expression. This expression cannot be confined within belief systems but is rather the exuberant expression of the heart.

134. Enjoy the Wonder of the Physical

Naktu-ararat-michta

Angel name: *Akta-misavi*

To one who expresses authentically and passionately, there are many things of great beauty he sees in his environment. The one who has limited self-expression sees many flaws. The reason for this is that the one who is not self-expressing, sees mostly backward images in the world around him, since his second set of inner mirrors are mostly not activated.

135. Luminosity through Authenticity

Nasur-biratresvi-skuchnava

Angel name: *Renehit-vilestrabit*

The real part of ourselves within the matrix cannot remember, and the rest of the ocean can only watch itself unfold through the 'magnifying glass' of the matrix, while not retaining anything, nor remembering anything. Without memory, wrong conclusions can be drawn, forming the illusions of existence.

136. Embracing Formlessness

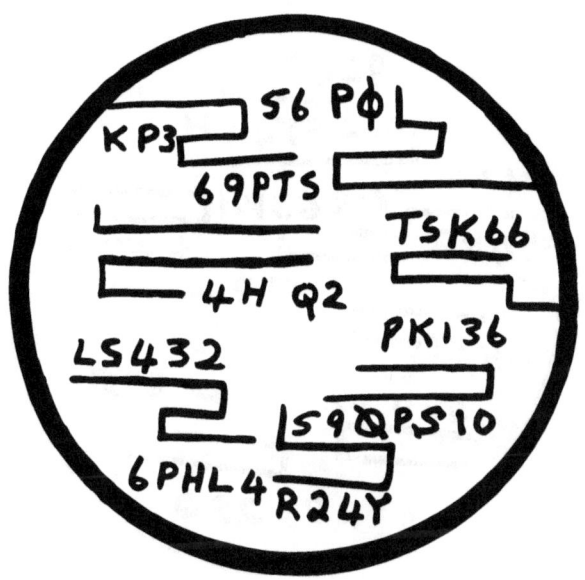

Halasur-nensetvalvi

Angel name: *Skipahur-nenesvi*

Our relationship with illusion (that which we are not) has gone through three stages: When first we experienced that which we are not in the mirrors of the matrix, we believed the lies, that it was really us. It caused fear and confusion. We could not understand why a specific intention would have an opposite effect.

137. Detecting Intrusion

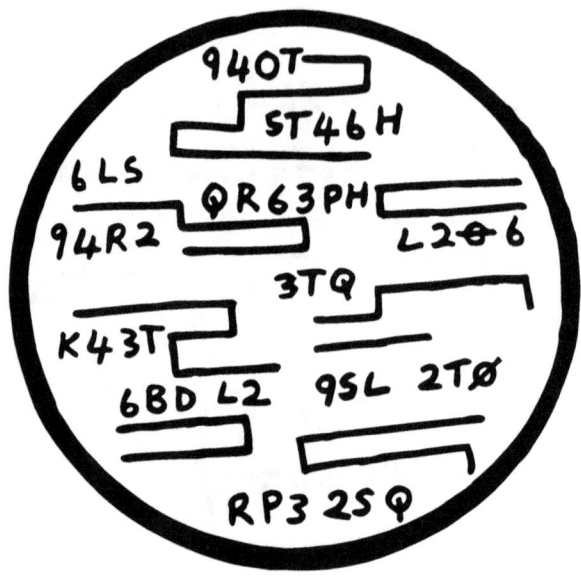

Rachbarut-sikharavesvi

Angel name: *Erektabit-eklar*

In the second stage, after having lost our innocence through eons of disillusionment, we have to acknowledge that we can know nothing. The matrix, having accumulated the data of experience, and being our opposite, claimed to know everything. At this point, the matrix changes from a tool of self-observation to a programmed dictatorship. For the individual, self-abandonment and disempowerment takes place.

138. Action Benefiting All

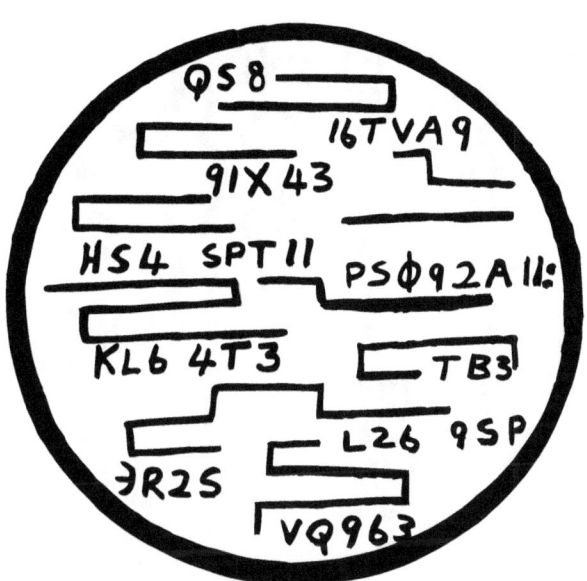

Nanbalsut-menensevi

Angel name: *Rutnatretvi-asur*

The third stage is the one very advanced beings of consciousness are in. They know the matrices of existence are unreal, but they are learning to take back their self-sovereignty and master the use of these tools. The evolutionary stages of someone in ego-identification are the exact replica of these vast evolutionary stages of life itself. (See the Evolutionary Stages of Man, page 110.)

139. Claiming Our Heritage

Skubarut-arsach-venevesvi

Angel name: *Rakbastur-ures*

When a tyrant is wounded and its despotic reign threatened, it becomes a raging persecutor. As the illusion of the tyrants of existence melts away, their efforts to get your attention will increase. Combat sudden aches and pains and disturbing dreams by asking:

1. What belief system do you have that allows their presence in your life?

2. What part of your existence is unexpressed that allows the belief system to exist?

140. Contentment through Surrender

Varut-pereve-huvrasat

Angel name: *Neshpa-prekprahur*

Shed now the last three judgments that block the achieving of the apex of understanding. For at the apex lies the door of everything, where eternity stretches into endlessness. The first judgment is based on the illusion of age. The second is based on the illusion of gender. The third judgment is based on the illusion of value.

141. The Infinite Moment

Kasanit-hilestra-brahut

Angel name: *Balavit-menenech-vavi*

Let the duality of speech be healed. Let your speech come from silence and let silence come from speech. When you speak, let it be the automatic communication of a silenced mind. When another speaks, let the words be received in silence that their intent may be felt in oneness with the speaker.

142. Greatness Through Self-Belief

Visterut-erekla-hersba

Angel name: *Kri-atar-pru-es*

In seeing the innocence of life and how all imperfection disappears as our perspective enlarges and becomes more inclusive, blame disappears. The concept of forgiveness likewise becomes meaningless. But forgiveness cannot be transcended until acceptance of the value of folly is in place. Only then can it be seen that unfolding eternal existence cannot be judged as acceptable or unacceptable from our very limited perspective.

143. Releasing Others to Their Journey

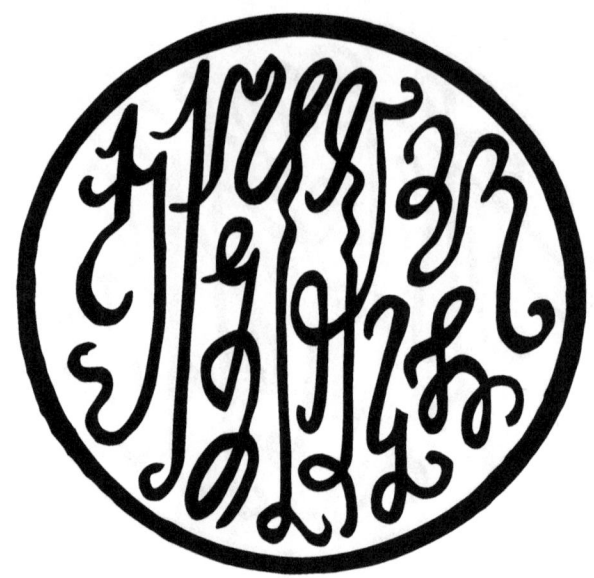

Nanuch-ubasetvi-uklet-harusat

Angel name: *Reksabit-plivarus*

We can refine our enjoyment of unfolding existence and emphasize certain aspects of it through our evermore, refined appreciation of it. Appreciation is the result of the full expression of our eternal being. When a deeper expression takes place, we find more to be grateful for; we awaken the poetic perspective.

144. Life from an Eternal Perspective

Meshenech-misavetvi-heresut

Angel name: *Arek-spababit*

In seeking to escape the matrix and its programs, we affirm its existence. We strengthen its illusion of being able to 'contain' and govern us. We strengthen its seeming hold on us as we try and escape it. The remembrance of our authentic essence and eternal being dissolves its dictatorial presence in our lives. When we express our authentic being one step at a time, guided by what evokes the poetry in our hearts, the matrix's grip releases.

Closing

The potent, magical essence of our being, that thunders through our veins and beckons us forth across imagined horizons, is ours to wield. Like the paints of vibrant colors an artist brings to life upon a canvas, we may fashion the magic of our lives into expressions of delight. Techniques can only dull the outcome with yesterday's mediocrity. It is upon the wings of a spontaneous heart that we can fly, unencumbered by programs of beliefs and unafraid of the limitlessness of our being.

Books by Almine

Irash Satva Yoga

Yoga, as a spiritual and physical discipline has been practiced in many variations by masters and novices for countless years and is universally accepted as one of the most effective development tools ever created.

Man's physical form in its original state was meant to be self-purifying, self-regenerating and self-transfiguring. Through pristine living and total surrender, it was possible to open gates in the body that would allow life to permeate and flow through it; indefinitely sustaining it.

In Irash Satva Yoga, received by Almine from the Angelic Kingdom, this ancient methodology is exponentially expanded and enhanced by incorporating the alchemies of sound and frequency.

Using easily mastered postures paired with music from Cosmic Sources created specifically for each, the 144 cardinal gates in the mind and body are opened and cleansed of their dross and debris, allowing the practitioner to tap into the abundance of the One Life.

Published: 2010, 94 pages, soft cover, 6 x 9, ISBN: 978-1-934070-95-6

Shrihat Satva Yoga

The human body is unique in that it is an exact microcosm of the macrocosm of created life. There are 12 points along the right, masculine side of the body and the same number on the left side. These are microcosmic replicas of the macrocosmic cycles of life.

The yoga postures are designed to open and remove the debris from these points – the gates of dreaming. This will occur physically through the postures and the music. Dissolving debris also occurs by way of dreaming (triggered by the breathing and eye movements), releasing past issues that caused the blockages in the points

Published 2010, 108 pages, soft cover, 6 x 9, ISBN: 978-1-934070-15-4

Saradesi Satva Yoga
The Yoga of Eternal Youth

As translated from the ancient texts of Saradesi – The Fountain of Youth. The ancient texts speak of time as movement. They affirm that time and space, movement and stillness, are illusions. To sustain any illusion requires an enormous amount of resources. This depletion of resources causes aging and decay. The illusion of polarity, the impossibility that the One Life can be divided and split is brought to resolution by balancing the opposite poles exactly. Only then can they cancel one another out, revealing an incorruptible reality that lies beyond – the reality of Eternal Youth.

Published 2011, 115 pages, soft cover, 6 x 9, ISBN: 978-1-936926-05-3

Books by Almine

Aranash Suba Yoga - The Yoga of Enlightenment

Almine's yoga for releasing trauma and strengthening the Eternal Song of the Infinite within.

Aranash Suba Yoga works at a deep core level to assist with releasing trauma, specifically through the effects that the postures, meditations and stretches have on the psoas muscle. This yoga turns its back on the illusions of the matrices and embraces the contradiction of an existence of no opposites. The overall benefit of *Aranash Suba Yoga* is to release the hold of illusion and strengthen the Eternal Song of the Infinite within.

Published: 2012, 116 pages, soft cover, 6 x 9, ISBN: 978-1-936926-50-3

Belvaspata, Angel Healing, Volume I
The Healing Modality of Miracles

Whether you are a beginner or an experienced master of the miraculous healing modality of Belvaspata, this comprehensive guide is an information rich handbook that will serve as your most valuable tool – a compendium of information for everything you need to know to establish yourself as a practitioner of this miraculous healing modality of the angels. Also included are Kaanish, Braamish Ananu and Song of the Self Belvaspata.

Published: 2011, 394 pages, soft cover, 6 x 9, ISBN: 978-1-936926-34-3

Belvaspata, Angel Healing, Volume 2
Healing through Oneness

Fairy Sound Elixir MP3 included

Whether you are a beginner or an experienced master of the miraculous healing modality of Belvaspata, this comprehensive guide is an information rich handbook that will serve as your most valuable tool – a compendium of information for everything you need to know to establish yourself as a practitioner of this miraculous healing modality of the angels. Belvaspata Volume II includes "The Integrated Use of Fragrance Alchemy," which delivers the method to obtain wellness of the emotional, mental and physical bodies through the combined use of Belvaspata, the alchemy of fragrance and the Atlantean Healing Sigils.

Published: 2012, 467 pages, soft cover, 6 x 9, ISBN: 978-1-936926-40-4

Books by Almine

Handbook for Healers
The Healing Wisdom of the Seer Almine

Handbook for Healers is an invaluable tool for anyone interested in self-healing or the healing of others. It offers both practical and spiritual guidance gleaned from the globally acclaimed Seer Almine's advice to her students during the past decade. It reveals vital information on rejuvenating the body and understanding its communication through the language of pain, and many more empowering insights.

Published: 2013, 648 pages, soft cover, 6 x 9, ISBN: 978-1-936926-44-2

Gift of the Unicorns
Sacred Secrets of Unicorn Magic, 3rd Edition NEW

Where have the Unicorns gone? And, what about mystical winged horses, mermaids, and giants – do they exist? The answers to all of our questions about these fabled creatures can be found in The Gift of the Unicorns.

This magical book tells the story of the Unicorns and Pegasus, and their heroism in preserving purity and innocence during the ages of darkness on Earth. In their own words, these beings reveal where they went, the purpose of their golden shoes and the sacred mission they undertook for the Mother of All Creation. What's more, they share long-held secrets about the Earth.

Published: 2012, 188 pages, soft cover, 6 x 9, ISBN: 978-1-936926-48-0

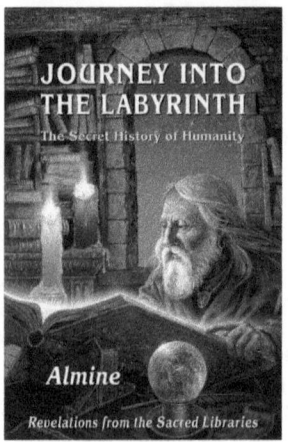

Journey Into the Labyrinth
Revelations from the Sacred Libraries

The online course *Revisiting the Labyrinth,* that has riveted truth-seekers from around the globe, is available now for the first time in book form. Disclosing the connection between the opening of hidden libraries and the awakening of the brain centers of man, this information packed book is bound to make a life-changing impact.

Journey into the Labyrinth details the forgotten role of the Earth and humanity, giving the reader new perspectives on the history of our species. Drawing from records from the hidden sacred libraries of Earth, lost civilizations and the wisdoms preserved by the indigenous peoples of the Earth, this book reveals a staggering older past then you may have ever imagined.

Published: 2012, 470 pages, soft cover, 6 x 9, ISBN: 978-1-936926-46-6

Books by Almine

Journey to the Heart of God
Second Edition
Mystical Keys to Immortal Mastery

Ground-breaking cosmology revealed for the first time, sheds new light on previous bodies of information such as the Torah, the I Ching and the Mayan Zolkien. The explanation of man's relationship as the microcosm as set out in the previous book A Life of Miracles, is expanded in a way never before addressed by New Age authors, giving new meaning and purpose to human life. Endorsed by an Astro-physicist from Cambridge University and a former NASA scientist, this book is foundational for readers at all levels of spiritual growth.

Published: 2009, 276 pages, soft cover, 6 x 9, ISBN: 978-1-934070-26-0

Secrets Of The Hidden Realms
Third Edition
Mystical Keys to the Unseen Worlds

This remarkable book delves into mysteries few mystics have ever revealed. It gives in detail:
- The practical application of the Goddess mysteries
- Secrets of the angelic realms
- The maps, alphabets, numerical systems of Lemuria, Atlantis, and the Inner Earth
- The Atlantean calender, accurate within 5 minutes
- The alphabet of the Akashic libraries.

Secrets of the Hidden Realms amazing bridge across the chasm that has separated humanity for eons from unseen realms.

Published: 2011, 412 pages, soft cover, 6 x 9, ISBN: 978-1-936926-38-1

The Ring of Truth
Third Edition
Sacred Secrets of the Goddess

As man slumbers in awareness, the nature of his reality has altered forever. As one of the most profound mystics of all time, Almine explains this dramatic shift in cosmic laws that is changing life on earth irrevocably. A powerful healing modality is presented to compensate for the changes in the laws regarding energy that healers have traditionally relied upon. The new principles of beneficial white magic and the massive changes in spiritual warriorship are meticulously explained.

Published: 2009, 260 pages, soft cover, 6 x 9, ISBN: 978-1-934070-28-4

Music by Almine

Children of the Sun

Music from the Known Planets (Re-mastered and re-titled version of the Interstellar Sound Elixirs)

The beautiful interstellar sound elixirs received and sung by Almine.

Price $9.95 MP3 Download
$14.95 CD

Labyrinth of the Moon

Music from the Hidden Planets (Re-titled version of the Sound Elixirs of the Hidden Planets)

All the vocals in these elixirs are received and sung in the moment by Almine

Price $9.95 MP3 Download
$14.95 CD

Jubilation - Songs of Praise

Music from around the world to lift the heart and inspire the listener.

The extraordinary mystical quality of the music, and the exquisite clarity of Almine's voice, creates the ambient impression of being in the presence of angels.

Price $9.95 MP3 Download
$14.95 CD

Visit Almine's website www.spiritualjourneys.com for world-wide retreat locations and dates, online courses, radio shows and more. Order one of Almine's many books, CDs or an instant download.
US toll-free phone: 1-877-552-5646

www.ingramcontent.com/pod-product-compliance
Lightning Source LLC
Chambersburg PA
CBHW060449170426
43199CB00011B/1141